The NIGHT That CHANGED Our LIVES

*The Devil Pushed Me In A Pit
But God Pulled Me Out*

KELLY GARNER

WESTBOW
PRESS®
A DIVISION OF THOMAS NELSON
& ZONDERVAN

Scripture taken from the Holy Bible, NEW INTERNATIONAL VERSION®. Copyright © 1973, 1978, 1984 by Biblica, Inc. All rights reserved worldwide. Used by permission. NEW INTERNATIONAL VERSION® and NIV® are registered trademarks of Biblica, Inc. Use of either trademark for the offering of goods or services requires the prior written consent of Biblica US, Inc.

Author Photo by Lee Walls

WestBow Press books may be ordered through booksellers or by contacting:

WestBow Press
A Division of Thomas Nelson & Zondervan
1663 Liberty Drive
Bloomington, IN 47403
www.westbowpress.com
1 (866) 928-1240

ISBN: 978-1-5127-0567-6 (sc)
ISBN: 978-1-5127-0569-0 (hc)
ISBN: 978-1-5127-0568-3 (e)

Library of Congress Control Number: 2015912154

Print information available on the last page.

WestBow Press rev. date: 7/31/2015

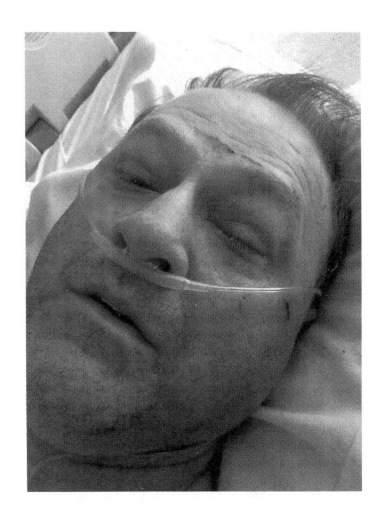

For he will command his angels concerning you
To guard you in all your ways …
"Because he loves me," says the LORD, "I will rescue him;
I will protect him, for he acknowledges my name.
He will call on me, and I will answer him;
I will be with him in trouble,
I will deliver him and honor him.
With long life I will satisfy him
and show him my salvation."

—Psalm 91:11, 14–16 NIV

"I am convinced that it was the grace of God that sent His protection &
mercies & angels for my brother Kelly while he spent 14-plus hours in the
8 degree cold, was severely injured, that he didn't aspirate on the blood he
was throwing up, that he didn't go into a diabetic coma, that his spinal
cord didn't snap in two when one of his thoracic vertebrae completely
obliterated leaving him paralyzed, and the hemorrhage in his brain has
not killed him.

"He's not out of danger yet, so please continue to mention
his name."

—Charlotte Garner Carter
Social media post, Snowmageddon 2014

Contents

Foreword

"Snowpocalypse 2014," they called the day when Birmingham, Alabama received two inches of snow and ice that shut down the entire city. The steep, hilly roads in the suburbs to the south led to abandoned cars and people waiting it out with strangers. The most memorable events, though, were of kindnesses and sacrifices offered to others to help-stores let people sleep in their building until loved ones could reach them, churches and schools kept kids all night until parents could reach them, and individuals risked life and limb to go out to help their neighbor. This is the story of one of those Samaritans.

Kelly Garner is a good man I didn't know other than by name, until that day. Later, as he began to attend my church after the experience described in this story. I began to know a man whose survival story got the attention of all of us. He can tell that story better than I, but it was all over the news, and still people recognize him as "hey, you're that guy!"

Kelly is more than "that guy," though. He almost died that night, but in some ways, he began to truly come alive that night. For Kelly, it was an awakening to life, to gratitude, and to God in a bewildering and wonderful way. He and his family went through testing, distress and helplessness that few will ever know to put life back together after it was almost taken away. And he found a deeper faith in God.

As dramatic as the rescue was, the journey since then is more important. Kelly is on the journey of becoming, one that invites us to live a new life and see it with new eyes. Such journeys roll out for many years after, and for them, it is still ongoing as we stumble forward, fall back, recover and re-learn many things again, and some for the first time. This is a good story, of a good man and his family, a man who went out one night to help, and never came back. It is one that all of us might live if we have eyes to see. I'm glad I met Kelly. You will be, too.

Dr. Gary A. Furr
Pastor, Vestavia Hills Baptist Church
Birmingham, Alabama

I've often heard people ask, 'Why does God let bad things happen to good people?' Ever since January 28, 2014, Kelly Garner has been asked that question many times. On that fateful night, Kelly says that the Devil pushed him into a ditch and God pulled him out. This book is not just the story of Kelly's recovery, but how a community came together to find him and how a city provided doctors and nurses to heal him. All of this is tied together by a belief that God can use any situation for good. Kelly's dilemma provides many lessons for us, and it's my hope that you will be encouraged to help others when you have the chance.

Life brings many challenges, but how we respond to them determines the kind of example we will set and the type of witness we will offer. Kelly responded to the challenges of that fateful day (and every day since) with a deep faith and a determination to make the best of whatever comes his way. His story is a powerful reflection of one man's faith and willpower.

As I sit writing this, I am watching the news and a story comes on about Kelly Garner. Today is the one-year anniversary of Kelly being released from the hospital. So I am not surprised that the news is covering his story again, but I am amazed at what they are reporting. Kelly has just finished the half-marathon at the annual Mercedes Marathon in downtown Birmingham. His surgical team ran with him. One year since his release from the hospital—and he has just ran 13.1 miles. I am amazed—or maybe I shouldn't be. What a miracle and what an inspiration.

—Jim Frazier, Minister to Boomers and Older Adults at
Vestavia Hills United Methodist Church.

Acknowlegemnets

This book would not have been possible without the love and support from my wife and two sons and from my sisters, brother and mother, my in-laws, and all the backing given from lots of individuals that are too numerous to name. They were there with their visits and phone calls checking on my status.

A special thanks for Maggie Keller and Jennifer Gerelds for helping me with the editing. They can tell you how grammatically incorrect I was many times. And to Dr. Gary Furr, Vestavia Hills Baptist Church, who put in some time to give me tips on writing my story. Also, a thanks for the book design from friend Rollina Oglesbey. She spent countless hours on this project and did a magnificent job.

The metro Birmingham media was there and was responsible for sharing my story and my face for all to see and be on the lookout. I have enjoyed time spent with each of the media outlets that have reached out to me and have become friends still today with several.

Many thanks to all the wonderful people who said a prayer for me and my family in our time of need. It was endless. It showed how intercessory prayer works. My family was fed for over 2 months by friends and neighbors with some fabulous meals. There were lots that answered the call out for help when the rescue party was formed. My neighbor had a big hand in the "finding" part, but to those that did go out to search and I have not said "thanks," I will never be able to thank you enough.

The neighbors and citizens of the metro Birmingham area, and my wonderful city of Vestavia Hills, Alabama, its first responders and law enforcement. My heartfelt thanks for the out pouring love and encouragement.

There were many messages with Bible verses shared with me as an encouragement and a spiritual message. While these verses are God's word, I purposefully placed many of these Bible verses in a section where I felt that message spoke to me and had that connection to the chapter. Thank you to those that did share these scriptures.

Prologue

The Night That Changed Our Lives

Tuesday, January 28, 2014, started out like any normal school day for my family. How could we know that an unforgettable nightmare was beginning ... one that would culminate in many miracles and change our lives forever? How could an accident that almost ended my life become instead a gift that touched and changed lives for months and years to come? Only by God's incredible grace. In the words of my favorite hymn, *Blessed Assurance, Jesus Is Mine*, "This is my story, this is my song: praising my Savior all the day long." Come along with me on a journey into a frozen night led by a desire to help, a life-threatening fall, and the miracles that followed.

Nine Lives

(Life with Type I Diabetes)

For those of you who don't know me personally, my name is Kelly Garner. I was born and raised in Florence, Alabama, and my life was just like everyone else's around me ... until I developed type 1 diabetes in 1975 when I was only nine years old. Basically, type 1 diabetes is a condition in which your own body attacks the beta cells in the pancreas, keeping it from being able to produce the insulin needed to process sugar in the blood. It might not sound like a big deal, but without the right balance of blood sugar in your system, you can go into a coma and even die if not treated.

Those with diabetes have to check their blood sugar levels regularly and understand some of the numbers that are associated with the disease. The normal range for blood glucose (blood sugar levels) is typically around 80–125 milligrams per deciliter. When a person drops below 80 mg/dl, it can start a decline known as hypoglycemia or low blood sugar. The opposite of this is hyperglycemia—when the blood sugar begins to climb above 125 mg/dl. When I was diagnosed in January 1975, my blood glucose rose to a whopping 2000 mg/dl and sent me into a comatose state for a couple of days. From those kinds of numbers, I soon realized that my life with diabetes would lead me down a rocky road.

Please do not allow me to strike fear in the hearts and minds of those with family members, especially children, who are coping with diabetes as I have. The events that I cover in this chapter are only my life's events and do not mean that you will go through these challenges I have had to endure, nor should you.

Whenever I talk about diabetes, I never let anyone think that they should feel sorry for me. I remind them every chance I get that many people are in a lot worse condition than me. I have lost many friends and family who battled cancer, and some are still in that fight for their life. Diabetes is very much a controllable situation that is maintained by lifestyle choices. Diabetics must put our hearts, minds, and souls into taking better care of ourselves with the right choices. I have had to come to this realization many times—sometimes too late. This, unfortunately, would be one of those moments.

The roller-coaster ride that can happen with diabetes has led me around some pretty steep curves in life, particularly the times I've hit a low while driving. This is a condition that has gotten many police departments and individuals with diabetes in deep trouble. There is nothing more horrifying than to be accused of being drunk when in actuality you might be in severe hypoglycemic mode.

Once, I was in a north Alabama city and found myself in that condition while driving, and I committed a hit-and-run. The victim did not know me or my condition beyond the fact that I hit his car and did not stop. Ironically, of all places, I parked several miles up the road in a liquor store parking lot. Pretty suspicious, I'd say, if I were a police officer answering this call.

Fortunately for me, the officer did not treat me as if I were a hardened criminal or a drunk driver. It also did not hurt that I already had my MedicAlert necklace out and dangling from my neck for him to see as he tapped on my car window to open up. This necklace, of course, identified who I was and what medical condition I have. The next memory I have is looking up from the ER bed with the staff attending to my needs and pumping an IV of dextrose 50 (helps first responders quickly get a low blood sugar to a stable level) into me. There beside me were my sister, Donna, and my mother looking over me. They took time off from their jobs and drove to Decatur General Hospital, from their town of Florence, Alabama, to be there for me.

I have had severe hypoglycemic moments, but this was the first time I was transported by ambulance due to my disease. Usually I am capable of handling it myself, or a friend, loved one or even a business colleague is there to help. One time, my wife could not wake me in the middle of the morning hours at our home. She knew that I was not in good condition. So much so, she loaded up a glucagon injection kit and prepped for this emergency injection. Glucagon is a hormone that causes the liver to release glucose into the blood. It is used to quickly increase blood sugar levels in diabetics with low blood sugar.

This is a drastic step, but it must be taken if a person with type-1, insulin-dependent diabetes is unconscious or does not respond immediately to the over-the-counter measures or food taken straight out of one's cupboard. She was not able to get it prepared before the Vestavia Hills Fire Medics were dispatched and arrived. I looked up from my bed to see four firefighters in our bedroom working to revive me. Their method of treatment was the dextrose 50 IV drip, which did not work quickly enough. They had administered two bags of this IV drip. Therefore, another ambulance transport was required.

05/21/2011

Garner Family 2011

Garner kids at Gulf Shores, AL, May 2014

Another one of those episodes took place during an unforgettable spring 2004, the season when I had the hit-and-run in Decatur. I then had a horrifying single-car accident in Mobile, Alabama. This was an accident that for hours caused my family back home in north-central Alabama to think I was dead. In hindsight, this seemed to foreshadow certain events close to ten years later.

Once again I became very disoriented because of a severe hypoglycemic episode. Fortunately for me, my accident this time involved only one car: mine. No other person was injured.

An eyewitness was mortified at what he saw take place. My car did three end-to-end flips and for good measure rolled twice. It was demolished. He said the scene reminded him of NASCAR, but he would not have hoped to see this up close and personal on a road he traveled daily. My car came to a stop upside down and caught fire. Luckily, a landscaping crew who had shovels tossed dirt onto the car to extinguish the fire. I was trapped inside my vehicle in such a way that there was no place to even check for a pulse.

This gentleman who saw my accident firsthand found something that was ejected from my car that had our name and phone number on it. He proceeded to call my wife in Vestavia, four hours away from Mobile, to give her the information that "your husband is dead." His intentions were almost admirable. But in retrospect, the call should have been handled by the Alabama State Troopers on the scene. He felt he was protecting her from the shocking "knock on the door" moment. I was airlifted to the USA (University of South Alabama) Medical Center in Mobile, Alabama, with what was believed to be a broken back and neck. Luckily for me, it was simply most of my ribs broken along with a shoulder and collar bone. I had always wanted to take a helicopter flight, but I can assure you that I hadn't planned it like this.

Kelly's car after May 2004 accident in Mobile

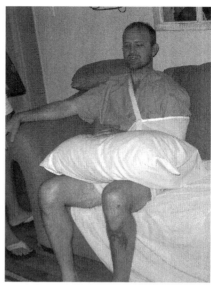

AL, Kelly's injuries showing up

I ended up in the ER, where I heard a familiar voice. I was relieved to know that the sibling love was alive and well. I woke to find my big brother, Mike, by my bedside, after having driven the hour-long journey from his home in Pensacola, Florida, to be there for me. Families are such a blessing from God! We do love and care about one another. My family once again would be there for me in my time of need as this January 2014 night unfolded. My tragedies have proven that sibling love is thriving and healthy, and I'm so thankful for it.

Another time in my life I had to have major reconstructive eye surgeries on both my eyes because of my diabetes. Dr. Rita Armitage diagnosed my rapidly declining eye condition immediately. Diabetic retinopathy was in its infancy. I was having what is known as floaters, bleeders, or worms in the eyes. This is blood vessel leakage that can cause permanent loss of eyesight. I thought then that I was finished and that I would never see my future kids grow up. I give Dr. Armitage all the credit for her professionalism during my time of uncertainty. I also give her big hugs on every return visit for saving my eyesight. She is one of my many heroes I'll be sharing with you.

Thankfully, I was referred to and was well taken care of by the Retina and Vitreous Associates of Alabama team of Drs. Robert Morris and C. Douglas Witherspoon. The world-renowned eye surgeons were able to correct my deteriorating condition. Removal of scar tissue was necessary for both eyes. Ever since, I have had a fear of possibly losing my eyesight permanently. I do know now that the high blood sugars I had growing up were due to the fact that we did not have the technology and equipment we have today, and this was the main cause for parts of my vision loss. In those days when I was first diagnosed with diabetes, we did not have Google. Information was a bit harder to get.

Another episode concerning my eyes took place as I was driving home from work one day and noticed that I no longer could see out of my left eye. It was a detached retina that nearly took my eyesight. I was on an operating table within an hour, where it was repaired and required weeks of recovery time. My recovery time for both eyes lasted over a year. I was told that some people have actually allowed a detached retina to go untreated so long that they are now permanently blind in that eye. I knew I had lots to be thankful for, having the world-class medical facilities that we have here in the Magic City of Birmingham.

Once a high school classmate saw me for the first time in years, and his reaction matched that of others: "So you are still alive? I thought you had died many years ago." Surprise, surprise. God has yet to call me home. I have lots left to do on this earth. It is now time for me to produce and find my ministry. And I am close to finding that place.

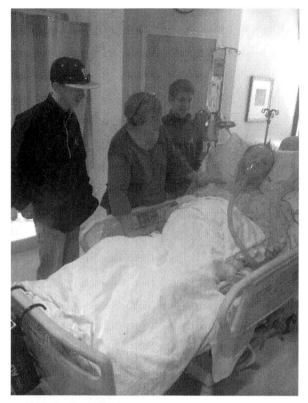

Kelly's family comforting him at his UAB Hospital
bedside, Melissa, Tyler, and Mitchell

These events, along with the one in early 2014, have traumatized my family. They have had to tolerate many such episodes and help me fight to get through them. I call these episodes diabetic demons. At first glance, having type 1 diabetes may seem tragic; it certainly has added drama, difficulty, and intrigue to what could have been an ordinary life. But God has a way of turning what appears terrible at first into a tool He uses to pour out His amazing love and grace on me and the people He puts in my path. And that's exactly what happened that fateful day in January 2014. I should have died, but God planned to turn another tragic event into an opportunity for hope and change.

Life's Tragedies ... God's Mercy

I have seen some tragedies in my life that I will not soon forget. The tragedies were losing two of my childhood friends in separate incidents. My friend Mark Berry was a kid I grew up with in the same neighborhood. Our friendship was formed while in our kindergarten years. We were swimming in our neighborhood swimming pool and bumped heads underwater and came up with fists drawn, ready to duke it out with one another. That near-fight led to years of friendship and growing up together.

Unfortunately, Mark's life was taken just two weeks after graduating from high school and just a few more weeks away from his eighteenth birthday. Mark had battled drug addiction for several years and was found dead early one summer morning after injecting some nasty stuff into his body. This was June 1983. A life cut short. His family hoped and prayed that if only one life could be saved because of his bad decision, Mark's untimely death might rescue someone from the gloom and doom he had encountered. He was a fine young man who got caught up in some of the bad habit-forming scenarios we all still see today and are faced with in our neighborhoods, schools, businesses, and churches.

Mark Berry   Brian Williams
7/31/65-6/13/83   3/21/64-2/3/98

The loss of my next friend to be called home came much later than when Mark's life was cut short. It was February 1998. Brian Williams was an awesome, free-spirited, loving individual who never met a stranger. He instantly became your friend once you met him. He was a good, wholesome Christian man, thirty-three years old. He had a spectacular family, and we did things together as families. We met at our home church in Florence, Alabama, Highland Baptist Church. Brian was a linesman for the Tennessee Valley Authority (TVA). He was struck and killed by a helicopter while moving power lines across the Tennessee River.

With Brian's death came a celebration of life. His life brought joy to many people's hearts. I had to ask a question once while we were sitting around talking with the Williams family reminiscing about Brian's life and what happiness he brought those who knew him. Knowing that it would bring a smile, I asked, "If once inside the pearly gates in heaven, would he see my dad or Bear Bryant first?" Brian was a huge Alabama fan, and the Bear was their legendary coach who had passed away in 1983 and a man Brian greatly admired and loved.

Mark and Brian were special friends who are sorely missed, but I know that God has two great men in heaven with Him.

Snowmageddon 2014

Times were already hard in January 2014. The company where I had been employed for over twelve years had suffered cutbacks, and I was among those they had to let go in order to stay afloat. I felt lost, unsure what lay ahead or what I needed to do in the present. One thing was for certain, though. I had developed carpal tunnel syndrome and was scheduled for surgery early in the morning. My wife, Melissa, and I pulled out of our garage on our short fifteen-minute drive to a 9:00 a.m. appointment that had been scheduled for weeks. Fasting was required for this procedure that I was about to go through. My last food or drink was around 9:00 p.m. the night before. Having type 1 diabetes and no nourishment would intensify the danger to come.

Driving northbound on Highway 31 through Vestavia Hills, we soon found ourselves in a heavy snowfall. It was remarkable how much the weather changed in five to ten minutes and over the course of a couple of miles. Our usually mild-weathered Alabama town quickly turned into a winter wonderland. Forecasters had assured us that there would be no accumulation—only snow flurries. They were off by about a hundred miles.

For those who don't know us Southerners, we aren't typically used to dealing with any form of snow or ice. However, I later read a letter of reflection about the wintry mix that day written by an out-of-town traveler here on business who lives with this type of weather six months out of the year. He wrote that our fiasco would have been more than even the most seasoned winter driver could have handled.

Later, weather forecasters informed us that the storm was more intense due to the warmer weather we had the weekend before. Many of us had been out in shorts and T-shirts over the weekend, but the nights dipped much lower, causing the ground to freeze. This caused the ground to turn the precipitation into a complete frozen tundra.

This had disaster written all over it for us in the South and particularly in the metro Birmingham area. We are used to only an occasional dusting of snow that does not cause that much trouble, if any at all. Our snowfalls that accumulate four inches are so rare that, like remembering a birthday or wedding anniversary, we can name where we were, how much fell and what year it took place. It sticks in your memory like where you were when hearing that JFK was shot or receiving word of the 9/11 catastrophe.

Snowstorms are so rare that we actually name them to correlate with the weather conditions that took place. I suppose that news organizations in every market do this, and we are no exception. This one for us would come to be known as *Snowpocalypse* to some or *Snowmageddon 2014* to others.

The suburb of Birmingham that we call home is named Vestavia Hills, and it has *Hills* in its name for good reason. Much of the city of Birmingham and surroundings are built up and over several mountains. If you're driving home from downtown Birmingham, you have to climb up, over, and down a mountain to get to the next suburb. Most people have even labeled the suburbs south of Birmingham as "over the mountain."

Melissa and I had not made it too far when we got a call from the surgery center telling us to turn around because they had canceled my procedure for this day. A drive home that would normally take us about five minutes on this day took at least an hour, and we still could not drive our car back to the house. We, too, became stranded motorists.

The snow came down fast and furiously, and the roadways quickly accumulated a tremendous amount of ice and snow. Our kids, Tyler and Mitchell, made it home safely from school. Melissa and I, meanwhile, were stuck at the entrance into our neighborhood.

We had no choice but to leave our car stranded there, along with the dozens of others around us. There was no way in and no way out by vehicle, because of the hills and curving roads. The slick surfaces caused many vehicles to begin blocking the neighborhood streets.

The main thoroughfare through Vestavia is a four-lane major road called US Highway 31 or Montgomery Highway. You can exit onto Highway 31 from Interstate 65 and drive a beeline into downtown Birmingham. From the city limits of Vestavia to downtown Vestavia, this stretch of the highway runs about three miles through our city, then another two miles through the suburb of Homewood until one reaches the downtown Birmingham area. This travel is mere minutes of driving.

During the day, Highway 31 is manageable enough, though hilly. At night, however, unless you know them well, the sections of Highway 31 that go through the two suburbs can be treacherous. They were very tough to tackle on a day like the one we were experiencing.

On the rare occasions when snow comes to the area, the interstate is likely shut down due to accidents. Unfortunately for some, many exited the interstate and tried to use Highway 31 as an alternate route. Unbeknownst to all of us hoping to make it a shortcut home, it turned into a slippery dead end. The roadway quickly became jam-packed with vehicles struggling for the right amount of traction to get them up the roadway and hopefully home.

Sadly, for many, this stretch of highway was as far as they would go. Besides, if they were trying to leave Vestavia Hills, it meant traveling a steep incline that lasts for several miles taking them right through the major bulk of the city's businesses and then an even sharper drop as they descend Shades Mountain to Brookwood Hospital, which is built literally on the side of Shades Mountain. This mountain is a part of the range of mountains that make up the southern end of the Appalachian Mountain Range and a part of the Cumberland Plateau.

By now the time was close to 11:00 a.m., and I was getting frustrated because I could not get our car home. I looked around and Highway 31 was a mere 100 yards away and was beginning to clog with cars, like some frigid parking lot up north. I know why people later dubbed it Snowmageddon. The scene looked like it was right out of the Bible: all empty vehicles with no live humans around.

Pictures in the newspapers and TV news stories showed vehicles stranded on every stretch of highway, byway, and interstate for miles. Many simply abandoned their vehicles in churches, schools, and business parking lots and on the side of roads. Even worse, some simply left them unattended right where they were stuck on the road. This caused some major worries for those who could maneuver their vehicles through it and for first responders trying to navigate through that mess.

Snowpocalypse scene in Birmingham,
Photo Courtesy of skybama.com

From almost every vantage point, the world had gone haywire. Gridlocked and freezing, the roads and the people trying to escape from them warned that all hell had broken loose. But at the same time, hope broke through. God, through strangers, poured out grace in the most unusual places and left an imprint that far outlasted the snow.

Snow Angels

There were dozens of people on foot and on all-terrain vehicles assisting all the motorists they could. The temperatures were now dipping close to single digits, and many individuals were already freezing cold.

I saw many volunteers pushing cars and some ATV operators out on this dreary day. These ATV drivers either helped pull small cars out of ditches or piggybacked someone so they could get kids home from school or family members home from work. All the people helping each other were a wonderful sight and fit me like a glove. It seemed like God had given us all a strong love for helping others whenever they needed it.

The kindness and caring were amazing. One story broke on the national news about how a neurosurgeon walked more than six miles in these horrible conditions to get to a hospital to operate on a critically injured person with a severe brain trauma. The walk took him more than three hours. This took place not far from the hospital where I would be transported. It was just one example of many absolutely incredible people with their genuine hearts of love who gave in time of need.

Many businesses, churches, and schools opened their doors to anyone who needed a place to crash and to be fed. In almost all instances they were fed for free, and one major grocery chain had customers with sleeping bags in the aisles as their "guests" for the night. That is what Birmingham, Alabama, and the state of Alabama are all about. The people of this city have been giving back to one another for many years through multiple tragedies, and this was to be one of those moments. Given Birmingham's history of generosity and benevolence in crisis, it should not have amazed me to hear that my town once again stepped up as it did.

For me, helping those on the roadway was not only about being there to help push their cars so they could get to where they wanted to be. I was simply enacting what I would have wanted someone to do for my own family members if they had been stranded. It would have meant a lot to me to know that a gentleman was there to direct one of the females in my life in the right direction. (Melissa has had to rib me many times before for helping someone in a time of peril, hoping that it would not cause my diabetes to get out of kilter. I remind her of these "helping the women in my life" moments and point out that this is my way of giving back to those in a time of need!)

In the past, I have often been out of town on business when moments like these have occurred. During the tragic tornado activity that hit the state of Alabama in April 2011, I was in San Francisco and horrified at what I was hearing about my home state more than 2,500 miles away. It was frustrating to be unable to help my family and my neighbors. Several knew I was gone and helped remove some trees from our yard that were blocking the street. A total of 238 people died in the state during this tragedy, including five University of Alabama students.

There were lots of motorists who stated that I was there for them on the road when they were stuck. Lieutenant Brian Gilham, Vestavia Hills Police Department Public Information Officer, mentioned my helping one vehicle driven by a pregnant lady who was having some trouble with her tires spinning out of control. This particular mom-to-be was far from her due date, so no need to worry—I was not asked, nor did I attempt to help deliver a baby in the backseat of a car with snow falling and temperatures dropping rapidly. That would have been more alarming than the actual chaos!

There were no other heroic measures on my part. I visited the Wal-Mart Neighborhood Market to grab a few bags of cat litter to help with the wheel traction and hot coffee for those needing to be warmed up while waiting in their cars. I recall giving most of the drivers some hope in this way. I was not looking for a pat on the back or a cake waiting for me the next day at my doorstep. John Wooden, Hall of Fame basketball coach at UCLA, once said, "You can't live a perfect day without doing something for someone who will never be able to repay you." Helping those in need was my pleasure.

So what had started out as a morning that I thought would be a quick, no-big-deal effort of moving a few cars out of the lane of traffic had now become one long day. I was just one of many who helped these hundreds of stranded motorists. It was hour after hour and car after car that now led to what would evolve into a hypoglycemic night for me.

Remember, I had been fasting due to the hand surgery that was scheduled for this day. My fasting continued through the course of the day. This is a bad idea for a person with type 1 diabetes. The thought of being hungry or my blood sugar dropping to a severe low never crossed my mind. I truly was more concerned for the well-being of those in need. I reasoned that my family was safe and sound, and I was not too far from our home. That's why I did not leave a note telling them where I had gone, truly believing that I would return home to a warm house later that night.

Into the Pit

Now that I had seen the last car make its way northbound on Highway 31, as far as police barricades would allow, I found an opportune time to relax. This resting place happened to be in a pickup truck parked in the median of the now deserted Highway 31. I popped open the tailgate, climbed into the empty bed of this truck, and flopped down on my back gazing at the stars, as more snow fell onto my motionless body and face. I had no idea that this would be the last truly wonderful feeling I would have in my back. It is surreal to understand now that the last time I would have an uninjured back would be at that moment staring up at the snowy sky.

I was totally exhausted. The low blood sugar woes began to set in fast. My oldest son, Tyler, reminded me of this as I answered his phone call around 7:00 p.m.: "Dad, where are you?" he asked. He knew from the sound of my empty voice that I was not in very good condition, the kind my family has witnessed one time too many. They knew from experience the answers that I was giving him meant that I was fading fast. I was acting a bit loopy. "Stay put, Dad," he instructed me. "We are on our way to help you home." The "we" was Tyler and his younger brother, Mitchell. Bullheaded by nature and now a little out of my mind, I decided that I could get myself home anyway.

Tyler and Mitchell spent the better part of that night and into the early morning hours the next day searching the sidewalks, the woods and "warming stations" in hope of finding me or at least someone who had seen their dad. In the meantime, Melissa was on the phone with family and neighbors searching for answers to my whereabouts. She also navigated through some of the neighborhood streets scouring the area for me.

> *He who dwells in the shelter of the Most High will rest in the shadow of the Almighty. I will say of the* LORD, *"He is my refuge and my fortress, my God in whom I trust." Surely he will save you from the fowler's snare and from the deadly pestilence.* **He will cover you with his feathers, and under his wings you will find refuge; his faithfulness will be your shield and rampart.** *You will not fear the terror of night, nor the arrow that flies by day .... Then no harm will befall you, no disaster will come near your tent.* **For he will command his angels concerning you to guard you in all your ways ....** **"Because he loves me,"** *says the* LORD, *I will rescue him; I will protect him, for he acknowledges my name. He will call upon me, and I will answer him;* **I will be with him in trouble ....**" *(Psalm 91:1–5, 10–11, 14–15)*

The events that took place next are a bit blurry for me. I was now in a hypoglycemic moment that was too severe —one that I will remember as *the* night that changed our lives forever. I stepped onto one of the sidewalks that run parallel to Highway 31 on both sides of this four-lane road. It was the path that leads back to my neighborhood. I could have easily gone left or right and still made it home from either direction. After those steps going forward, I do not recall a thing.

Some have speculated that I simply stumbled and plummeted forty feet off an embankment, hitting my head on the way down the ravine and landing in a dried-up creek bed. Sprawled wide open, my body dropped and my back happened to find the biggest, flattest boulder in the entire, massive canyon, shattering the vertebrae that made direct contact. Had the stones been smaller, more jagged, I simply would have suffered major lacerations. Perhaps they would even have cut me in two.

This area where I landed sits just behind the Vestavia Hills "Library in the Forest." The entire wooded area is known as Boulder Canyon and is reminiscent of a cereal bowl. There are similar drop-offs on an adjacent stretch of road that comes and goes out of my neighborhood.

Boulder Canyon is Vestavia's hiking gem—a mix of steep climbs with flat ridge and creekside paths. This scenic trail is just yards away from busy US Highway 31. This twelve-acre area is where the trail's humble beginnings can be traced to the efforts of sixth-grader Barney Wilborn and three separate Eagle Scout projects. The walking trail covers more than a mile and a half. It has support from other area Boy Scout members, Keep Vestavia Green and the Rotary Club.

With shattered vertebrae, I was nearly paralyzed. The injury came inches from severing my spinal cord. Later, the announcement to my family of this near miss was deemed, by the surgeon who pieced me back together, a true miracle. He likened the shattered pieces of my vertebrae to crumbled fragments of crackers. (I jokingly asked him later whether he super-glued me back together.)

In this dark, snow-covered ravine, I lay unconscious for more than twelve hours in reportedly eight-degree temperatures all night. It should have been my last.

Saving Grace ... and Social Media

My family now had not heard from me in more than an hour and was out looking for me. My wife was on the phone with anyone who could give her direction as to what to do. Some speculated that I had done what many had to do that night—seek shelter at one of the many businesses, churches, and schools that had opened their doors to hundreds as "warming stations." Obvious only to me, this was not the case, unfortunately. My poor family faced the sheer terror of the unknown. "Where is Kelly, what could he have done?" they worried.

My wife and boys, my sisters and brother and mother started an all-night campaign to get the word out that their husband, dad, brother, and son had gone AWOL. *PLEASE HELP!* It was only a bit more than an hour after my last phone conversation with my family. To my amazement, I was considered missing, albeit the social media version of "missing." Later, I was surprised to find that they had jumped to action so quickly, considering the "child is missing after twenty-four hours" rule. But it's amazing what a positive tool social media can be, as it was for me that night. My sister Charlotte's Twitter and Facebook onslaught caught fire, with exponentially growing attention that could have made Mark Zuckerberg jealous.

She had luck reaching out to every news organization, police, and fire rescue web thread and had every friend and their friends "share" the fact that I was missing. She was able to get my picture plastered on every possible social media site known to mankind.

21

A friend and former employee of one of my accounts, Ashley Watts Gaithers, posted this message for her friends to see: "Police asking for help finding man last seen around 7 p.m. in Vestavia Hills. Oh my goodness, I know him very well!! He was our FreeStyle Diabetic Supplies rep @ Professional Apothecary for many years!! This guy is genuine and has a heart of gold. He is a really bad diabetic himself. His wife is a pharmacist. I hope he has since been found, but help pass this along just in case! Prayers are with him and his family!!"

A year later, during my "recovery anniversary," Ashley went on to say: "So happy Kelly was found safe! He is the good Samaritan who risked his own life to help others during the treacherous ice & snow last year. I've never known Kelly to meet a stranger; he is a friend to all, even those strangers in need!"

Many times I had come close to shutting down a couple of my online accounts and turning my attention to something more positive! I had found myself getting into online written arguments, sometimes with complete strangers. There was nothing I could say or do to change someone's point of view. Now, in hindsight, the best thing one can do for another is to kneel down to pray for that individual. This would be the best use of time, not debating with some stranger when you might well be disagreeing with your own grandmother on the other end of the exchange. There has to be a better way to spend quality time than on a computer all day and night!

On January 28, around 10:30 p.m., my mother got a phone call from my sister Donna. My mother had just dropped off to sleep. She knew something was wrong from Donna's voice. She told our mom that I was missing. All kinds of thoughts ran through Mom's head. "Was he kidnapped, or what?" she wondered. She got up, went into the den, and picked up her Daily Devotion. She opened up to Psalms and read, "I cried out to the Lord and He heard my cry."

Mom later said, "I thought, wherever Kelly is, God, Kelly is calling out to You. You know where he is, and his family doesn't." She said she felt she had to tell someone. She called a friend and told her to start praying for Kelly. The prayer chain began cranking up. Another friend insisted on being there with her should she get some bad news. They were up all night praying and texting my brother and sisters and Melissa and the boys, trying to keep in touch and to make sense of all that was going on.

With the weather so bad in Birmingham, she could not travel to help look for me. She said her thoughts were that I had gotten into a stranded car or gone to someone else's house. Mom never felt they would find me dead. As typical as my mother is, she had that wonderful peace about the situation that can come only from God.

A little after 8:30 the next morning came the good news. I had been found and was alive! Not knowing what kind of condition I was in, Mom gave God all the praise and glory for keeping me safe through the freezing weather.

During her time of waiting and praying for the unknown whereabouts of her son, Mom meditated on the following Psalm. (I still have the verse she clipped out of her prayer book for me to have in the hospital. It was more than foretelling for God and His angels to have this verse ready for my mom in that time of comfort while I lay in the pit, right?)

> *I waited patiently for the LORD; he turned to me and heard my cry. He lifted me out of the slimy **pit**, out of the mud and mire; he set my feet on a **rock** and gave me a firm place to stand. He put a new song in my mouth, a hymn of praise to our God. Many will see and fear and put their trust in the LORD.* (Psalm 40:1–3)

By now my two sons had started searching from one shelter to the next, at any place that might resemble a bunker for the night, to see if I was stashed there. They bought candy bars to put in their pockets just in case they found me wandering around on the roads heading back to our house. These were my quick-fix chocolates that have saved me many times during a low-blood-sugar episode.

Of all people they ran into, while inside our local Wal-Mart Neighborhood Market, was a friend of ours who is the director of the Vestavia Hills Public Services Department, Brian Davis, and with him was a city police officer. Brian was there making a snack run for a couple of the city-run storm shelters. My boys asked him if he had seen their dad. He then reminded them of the text I had sent to him in the early hours of the storm asking if the city employees had this thing under control. I told him I would be more than happy to be of some help. He simply responded that they had all the help they needed, and I should stay put. Funny thing happened. Well, in hindsight, it wasn't that funny. I didn't listen to him and didn't stay put. If only I had listened, because my day and night was about to get much worse.

> *A new command I give you: Love one another. As I have loved you, so you must love one another. By this all men will know that you are my disciples, if you love one another.* (John 13:34–35)

I told you there were many heroes in my life. My neighbors Steve and Sheila Bendall are two of them. They read the sites on Facebook and saw the TV news channels the next morning about all those missing from the storm, and my picture was one of the many that was on every news outlet. They formed a daybreak search party that panned out all over Vestavia Hills. Word circulated about what they were doing, and it got even bigger and farther away from the Hwy 31 corridor.

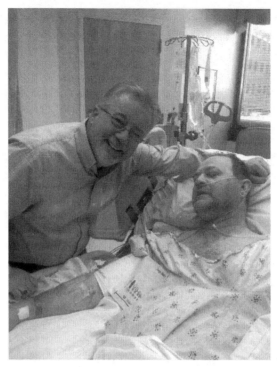

Visiting Kelly's bedside, family friend and WestBow author,
Roger Mardis, *Big Doors Swing on Small Hinges*

In the meantime, on multiple social media sites thousands were leaving
messages of thoughts and prayers for my family and me in hopes of finding
me alive and well. Unfortunately, there were some unkind words being
passed around through the cyber world asking why I was being singled
out as missing and was getting all the publicity. Many even thought I must
be a "suspect" if the police were on the lookout for me. In their defense,
quite a few had yet to make it home that night and were unable to call,
leaving their loved ones worried, as well. There were dead cell phones, as
well as dead car batteries, all over the city. I will give my family all the
credit for pushing the right buttons and starting the process of labeling
me as "missing."

The search party idea worked, as my neighbor Mike Shofner was on foot
with a Vestavia Hills police officer heading north on the Highway 31
sidewalk nearing the Vestavia Hills Library. They were paired up to make

it easier on the search. They scoured the neighborhood out to the highway. There Mike was perplexed as he looked over a section of guardrail near the sidewalk and noticed something that did not belong—what looked like a pair of blue jeans. Mike yelled down to where I and my broken back were resting on this boulder, "Kelly, is that you?"

My answer was a simple "yes." Mike says I answered with my eyes popped open and a grin on my face. By this time, Mike and the police officer were separated.

I received hours of radio traffic calls that were made throughout the night and into the early morning hours. These were police calls made between patrolmen/women to the radio room, giving details of their changing location while they looked for me. These calls were ultimately passed on to the Vestavia Hills Fire and Rescue. The 911 dispatcher had been inundated with calls all through that wintry night seeking help. So when the dispatcher received Mike's call, it took a while to clarify that I had indeed been found and needed immediate help. This is the transcript of the 911 call that Mike made from his cell phone as he was covering me and comforting me, doing his best to help me stay warm.

> *911 Dispatcher:* **Is this an emergency?**

> *Mike:* **It is indeed. We are south of 31 [Highway 31] behind the library, down in the ravine, we have a body that is severely injured, fell down the hill last night, he has been out here all night.**

> *911:* **Okay, like in a car wreck?**

> *Mike:* **It is a missing person, my neighbor Kelly … Garner, I'm his neighbor.**

> *911:* **The person that has been missing since last night?**

> *Mike:* **Yes, he has been reported missing. He fell down the ravine last night. He looks like he has taken a pretty bad**

blow to the head, there is a lot of blood on a rock, but he is conscious. — Stay with me, Kelly, look at me, Kelly, and don't close your eyes.

911: [lots of typing heard in background from 911 dispatcher] What is his name again?

Mike: His name is Kelly Garner.

911: Was he reported missing to the police?

Mike: Yes, he was.

911: How old is he?

Mike: Kelly, how old are you? Kelly, stay with me. — He has diabetes. [I was told by Mike but could not hear it on audio that when he asked me my age, I told him that I was twenty-three. *In actuality, I was forty-eight years old.*]

[Mike is heard speaking with others at the top of the hill] He's alive, he's hypothermic.

911: Okay, he is responding to you, just not very well?

Mike: [he is heard speaking with me] Come on, Kelly, stay with me, ugh, gasping for air as it is awful cold ... [Some gurgling noises in the background can be heard coming from me.] No, he is not responding very well.

911: Do you have any blankets, coats that you can cover him up with?

Mike: I have my coat on him, my toboggan on him.

911: Did he wreck a vehicle, or was he walking or what?

[Mike is heard telling others on the topside not to come down because of all of the rocks, very icy.]

911: You say he is down in a ravine?

Mike: Yeah, he is right down here.

911: All right, was he in a vehicle then, or was he on foot?

[Mike now heard asking others at top of hill] Do you have any blankets or anything, throw them down here—he's been down here all night.

911: Was he in a vehicle or was he on foot?

Mike: He was on foot, and he went walking down this hill and like I said, he has diabetes, so it must have gotten out of whack.

911: Do you see any other injuries?

Mike: There is dry blood right next to his head on the rock he is lying on.

[Again to those attempting to come down from topside] Here, here, what is your name? He is the missing person we have been searching for. Grab this rope and ride it down slowly, hold on to it tight. — Kelly, stay put, don't move. He has gashes all over his forehead.

911: Don't try to move him in any way; keep him covered the best you can. — I do see that you are just south of Roundhill Road, behind the library. Don't move him in any way. We have fire and rescue and law enforcement on their way to your location.

Mike: **We have multiple folks here to help—thanks a bunch.**

This is another one of the radio traffic calls that went out that morning from the fire department:

Vestavia Hills Fire Dispatcher: **[Alarm sounds, bells ring] Rescue 31, Battalion 1, respond to Montgomery Highway and Roundhill Road. Call for a traumatic injury; it is the missing person from last day.**

VHFD Dispatcher: **Rescue 31, battalion 1, be aware that PD is advising that patient will need to be moved a great distance out of ravine to rescue unit. Additional rope might be needed.**

This is from a social media site that had been set up, dedicated to help keep those interested in my whereabouts in the loop, and to give a place to post if I had been seen and where:

KELLY HAS BEEN FOUND!! He fell into the ravine behind Central. Search party found and they are pulling him out now. He is alive and conscious and talking. THANK YOU to everyone who helped!!

In the interim, Steve Bendall began a rapid descent to my location on his rear end to reach me as quickly as possible, while his wife, Sheila, scurried to locate some blankets to wrap and keep me warm, as they all knew that I was in grim condition and more than likely suffering from extreme hypothermia. The idea that I came out with no signs of any frostbite is truly miraculous. Firmly believing that God does intervene, I consider it evidence that God just still has more plans for me around here! And there are plenty of miracles to pass around.

A multitude of individuals were helping extract me out of the wooded area of the ravine. The Vestavia Hills Fire and Rescue arrived on the scene and began an assessment of my condition and put a cervical collar on because of the drop I had made and the likelihood that I would have some neck injuries. They later said that I was able to tell them where my pain was, and a backboard was brought onto the scene. This was a good thing, considering that the surgical team said a wrong move could have produced severe repercussions. Though I was conscious enough to report my pain, I could not recall anything that had happened that night before, when I had walked about a mile and a half along Highway 31. This is the distance I would have covered up and down this stretch of highway. I could have walked five steps or five hundred. I had no recollection of anything that had taken place.

The hike out of the woods was not a very fun or easy task for this group. They had to start a daisy chain system, because the snow and ice made it very slippery to get me out. They had a convoy of two on each side of the backboard, while the other four moved forward waiting for the group with the board to arrive.

Once they passed about a hundred yards of wooded area, they made it to a clearing where another neighbor had an ATV awaiting my arrival. They strapped me to the back of it, bringing me out another two hundred yards, where an ambulance equipped with snow chains was ready to take me away. It was the only ambulance with snow chains the city had that day.

I am with Vestavia Hills Fire Medics, Corey Sumner, Steven Michael, & Alan Bates, standing on the actual rock where I landed and was extracted from

The first plan was to hoist me out via a hook and ladder engine or by a private construction crane or perhaps even a wrecker. These were only one or two other options, depending on availability and if they could fit through the crowded roadways. My neighbors had a plan in place and began the extraction with the Fire Medics using the ATV. It was exhausting work due to the weight of the equipment and my weight, coupled with the slippery ground and the distance out of the ravine and wooded area.

> Love must be sincere. Hate what is evil; cling to what is good. Be devoted to one another in brotherly love. Honor one another above yourselves. Never be lacking in zeal, but keep your spiritual fervor, serving the Lord. Be joyful in hope, patient in affliction, faithful in prayer. Share with God's people who are in need. Practice hospitality. (Romans 12:9–13)

Those who know how rabid we are about college football in the state of Alabama, specifically about our two largest universities, know that they are the fiercest of rivals. They both have had their share of glory recently with championships being passed around. Ironically, many of the neighbors who were on the scene first and took charge of my extraction from the ravine were Auburn University fans who rescued a huge University of Alabama fan (me) who also happened to have earned a degree from Auburn. That is all fine and good, as long as the other side holds no grudges. The rivalry was put on hold, at least for a couple of days.

This reminds me of the assassination attempt against President Ronald Reagan in 1981. Going into surgery to remove a bullet that is lodged near his lungs that could have easily been pushed to his aorta causing certain death, he quipped to one of the surgeons about to operate on him, "I sure hope all of you doctors are Republicans!" Of course there was a quick laugh and the surgical team response was that it didn't matter right now. To the dismay of many college football antagonists and talking heads, Alabama and Auburn fans are truly there for each other in time of need.

Each time one of Auburn's athletic teams, notably the football team, wins a game; the Toomer's Corner oak trees are rolled with toilet paper. The Alabama faithful reached out with a donation website to help pay for and restore the oaks that were poisoned in winter of 2010 and destroyed by a so-called zealot 'Bama fan who was later charged with this crime. In return, Auburn supporters were there for the Tuscaloosa residents in April 2011 when a massive and deadly tornado ripped through many parts of the state, including Tuscaloosa. This tornado killed five University of Alabama students.

Thankfully for me, there was no argument about which college team I root for. War Eagle and Roll, Tide, Roll!

> *"The Lord bless you and keep you; the Lord make his face shine upon you and be gracious to you; the Lord turn his face toward you and give you peace." So they will put my name on the Israelites, and I will bless them.* (Numbers 6:24–27)

My boys were able to get a ride with a friend's dad, and my sister Charlotte and her husband, Hank, traveled in the snow and ice across town in their four-by-four truck and stayed with me throughout the entire ordeal. My wife was being ushered to the hospital by the generosity of the Vestavia Hills Police Department. The rest of my family lives out of town, and the roads weren't navigable for a couple of days. Because some interstate roads were nearly impassable, a few members of my family took almost eight hours to travel a normally three-hour trip.

One neighbor had a friend who worked in an office complex overlooking the library and had a good view of this team bringing me out in the open. All she could see out of her office window, however, was an individual covered from head to toe. It was reminiscent of a body bag leaving the scene. My neighbor had to explain to her friend that this was not the case, or rather it should not be. Her son was the one driving the ATV that brought me out of the woods behind the library, and the last she had heard from him was that I was alive but not doing well.

Kelly with his St. Vincent's Hospital ER team, the
first to treat me after being transported

Cheryl Chastain, RN, Dr. Larry Wade, Ashley Faulkner, RN

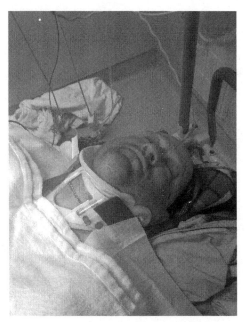

One of the first pictures my sister Charlotte
took of me at the St. Vincent's ER

I was taken to a hospital that was a short drive from my home where they did a complete scan and discovered how extensive my injuries were. They had to transport me to a level 1 trauma center because the first hospital was not equipped for that amount of injury. The trauma unit happened to be about three miles down the road in downtown Birmingham.

Reflections

These are just a few individuals who mean a lot to me and were a part of my journey. They took time to share what this night and my ultimate rehabilitation was like for them to witness.

Light flurries began to fall. Forecasters in Birmingham predicted a light dusting for January 28, 2014. And that's exactly what happened. That is until roads began to ice over, crippling the city. Traffic accidents on major interstates and thoroughfares jammed up the roads, leaving many drivers stranded in their cars.

The snow began falling around 10 a.m. As hours ticked by people began abandoning their cars to seek shelter, many of them miles from home. Many parents were not able to pick up their children from school. Parents spent the night at work. Kids spent the night with their teachers and classmates. I guarantee most people will not forget where they were during "snowmageddon" or "snowpocalypse" as it became dubbed on social media.

I had been out covering a story early that morning. I eventually made my way back to the television station and went straight to work answering phones, editing video, anything I could do to contribute to our wall-to-wall coverage of the winter weather.

Stories began to flood into our newsroom. There were many calls for help. Around 7 p.m. that night, our station received an email from Vestavia Hills Police. They were asking for assistance finding a missing man. His name was Kelly Garner. Police told us he had been out on Highway 31 assisting drivers who were stranded. They were concerned about him because the sun was going down, temperatures were dropping, and his family hadn't heard from him. He was also a diabetic and needed his insulin. I'm not sure why his story stuck out to me among the rest. Perhaps it's because I'm from Vestavia Hills as well and we have several mutual friends, although I had not met Kelly prior to this story. Whatever it was, something compelled me to dig into this story further.

Our television station put the information on TV. We showed it several times throughout the night. As we signed off around midnight, there was still no word on the missing man—the Good Samaritan, as he was being called.

Everyone who was at the station spent the night because it was too dangerous to drive down the icy, snowy hill. After a few hours of sleep, we began preparing for our morning show broadcast at 4:30 a.m. We recapped all of the stories about people stranded overnight. We were hearing wonderful stories of people helping strangers, neighbors helping neighbors, and communities pulling together, but still no word on Kelly Garner.

It wasn't until daylight we got word he had been found. Police confirmed to us Kelly had fallen down a ravine near the library on Highway 31, where he had last been seen helping stranded drivers. The Good Samaritan was alive but in critical condition. It was an answer to many prayers.

Throughout the day I was in contact with Kelly's sister Charlotte, in Mountain Brook, AL. She was sending me pictures and information about Kelly. She was keeping me updated on his condition and prognosis.

As our winter weather coverage continued, we continued to share the story about the missing Good Samaritan who had been found alive. It was a story that captured the hearts of many of our viewers. But at that time, we didn't know the entire story about this man. We didn't know who Kelly Garner was. We didn't know what else he had been through prior to this accident.

Several weeks later, UAB Hospital, where Kelly had been recovering, invited the media to interview Kelly and the doctors who treated him. I covered that story and continued to have so many questions about how this man survived. First it was a miracle he survived the fall; second it was a miracle he survived in the freezing temperatures. The only explanation that makes sense to me is that God was with him through it all.

In an ironic twist, on the one year anniversary of the Snowpocalypse, my mother was watching a live remote I conducted with Kelly at the scene of his collapse. She sent me a message that she recognized him as the man who helped her on that January 2014 night.

—Clare Huddleston, WBRC Fox 6 News Reporter,
Birmingham, Alabama.

* * *

As you read Kelly's story and his testimony, I hope you can see Jesus through him. I hope his words inspire you and they have inspired me and others he has met.

In my 22 years of law enforcement experience I don't recall an incident in which I felt as challenged.

At approximately 11:30 a.m., on January 28, 2014, our city of Vestavia Hills and surrounding region were abruptly mired in an unexpected labyrinth of snow and ice. Seemingly thousands of people were in need or calling for help. The temperatures for the night were forecast to drop into single digits, and many were still stranded in their vehicles or in unlikely shelters. As the day turned to dusk, I recall praying, "God, don't let anyone die tonight; that's all I ask, no one dies."

Then a mid-evening call came from a co-worker in regard to a missing local man who suffered from severe diabetes. He was last seen hours earlier helping motorists stuck in the snow. He explained that his name was Kelly Garner, and his family was desperately seeking for him. We dispatched officer after officer to attempt to locate him at any of the makeshift shelters that had sprung up in our city and searched abandoned cars in the vicinity he was last seen, all to no avail. We pinged his phone, posted him on our social media, and requested local news affiliates to share. Our hope, everyone's hope, was that he had found shelter somewhere for the night and had simply lost cell service. But as the night dragged on, it became very apparent that was unlikely the case.

We received a multitude of calls that night; however, call it what you would like, premonition, intuition, gut instinct; something about this one seemed different. Words can't appropriately explain it; however, something about this situation seemed immeasurably daunting. The vastness of the miring snow and ice, our response limitations posed by hampered transportation, the frigid temperatures, and the continuous onslaught of calls from those requesting our help, all compounded the gnawing in my stomach that, without a miracle, Mr. Garner's situation was not likely to end well.

Just as the morning sun peeked over the frozen landscape, exhaustion was setting in from a very long night. The news came that Mr. Garner's neighbors banded together at first light in search of him. They had located him alive in a deep ravine just off the main highway through our city.

Miracles do happen!

Astounded was an understatement. In consideration of the environment and for the length of time he was exposed, God's hand, grace, and protection were undeniable. I uttered a meek thank you to Him for answering my prayer.

Since that day, Mr. Garner's spirit and perseverance through recovery should serve as a testament of God's will, ultimate plan, and authority for each of our lives. Take the time to read his remarkable story and journey. You will be touched, humbled, and inspired.

—Vestavia Hills Police Department Public Information Officer, Lieutenant Brian Gilham

* * *

The night of January 28, 2014, stands out in the minds of emergency responders from throughout central Alabama. While each winter weather event in our area causes disruption, discomfort, and inconvenience, that night was remarkable because of its suddenness and drastic impacts. The ice and snow that Tuesday left hundreds stranded; not merely inconvenienced but imperiled. For many committed public servants, it was the first time they could not access those who depend upon them. 911 lines rang throughout the night, and busy fire and police radios reported efforts to help those in need and account for the missing.

During all of that, Kelly Garner lay on a rock injured and fading, but he wasn't alone. Kelly's faith was sustaining him while his neighbors and emergency responders looked for him throughout the night. When located, his physical condition was precarious although his trust in the Lord was unwavering.

The results of Kelly's desperate situation at the bottom of a ravine drew much attention from broadcast and social media alike. His recovery was long and painful and his story serves as a reminder for us: "Trust in the Lord with all your heart, and lean not on your own understanding; In all your ways acknowledge Him, and He shall direct your paths." Proverbs 3:5–6.

—Jim St. John, Fire Chief, Vestavia Hills, Alabama

* * *

With all that was going on when the surprise ice storm slammed Central Alabama on January 28, 2014, it was hard not to be captivated by the story of Kelly Garner. First, there was the search for him in the midst of the unending chaos in that instantly icy world—the Good Samaritan now himself in need of help. There was the moment of relief when word spread that he had been found. For many of us, it seemed a perfect, inspiring bookend to one family's anguish and in this era of instant media, we moved on. If only it were that simple. Being brought out of the ravine was just the first stride in a steady hurdle race that continued away from the spotlight, as a man relearned some of the daily tasks we take for granted with the goal of fully mending himself, buoyed by the love and support of family, friends, and strangers touched by his ordeal.

This is that story, in his own words, of the arduous personal, physical, and spiritual journey that could understandably shake anyone's faith. It has only made Kelly Garner's stronger.

—Mike D. Smith, Writer.

* * *

Once in a great while, there's a story with the power to educate, entertain, and inspire. In Kelly Garner's miraculous survival against the odds, you will be taken on a compelling journey. It begins with a man's selfless desire to help people during a surprise winter storm. Kelly's noble efforts, however, meet with an unpredictable turn, culminating in a life or death struggle. Kelly's unlikely survival and recovery have inspired people around the world. In the process, Kelly finds that God's plan for his life has been revealed. His remarkable story demonstrates that we are not defined not by the obstacles we face, but how we respond.

—Jim Faherty, News Radio 105.5
WERC, Birmingham, Alabama.

* * *

I first met Kelly Garner after a devastating snowstorm paralyzed Birmingham, Alabama, January 28, 2014. It was a one-sided meeting. Kelly was unconscious, a patient in intensive care at the University of Alabama at Birmingham Hospital where I work in public relations.

Kelly had spent the day of the storm assisting stranded motorists. He spent the night lying in the freezing cold at the bottom of a ravine after tumbling some forty feet down the slope while on his way home.

I got to know him during his month at UAB Hospital, fielding endless phone calls from news media reporting on his recovery from spinal, neck, head, and rib injuries. As the day of his hospital release loomed, Kelly told me he wanted to say thank you to the legions of friends and admirers who had followed his recovery and who had offered their support to this man who was so rightly called a hero.

We brought in reporters and camera crews on the day of his discharge. His rehab physician was on hand to answer medical questions. The hall was thronged with nurses, therapists, and hospital staff who gathered to see him off. Kelly came into the room with bountiful optimism, a huge smile, and a message. A message of hope, of perseverance, and of strength. He was indeed a hero on January 28. As you'll see in the pages of this book, that was just a beginning.

—Bob Shepard, University of Alabama at Birmingham.

* * *

All the weather forecasters said, "snow flurries with no accumulation in the Birmingham area." If you are from Alabama, *snow* is a four-letter word meaning "go buy all the bread and milk you can." Most of the time people joke about the rush to the grocery store. That day in January would be different. About 9:00 a.m. the flurries turned into an all-out winter storm, and the rush to try and get home from work and school snarled traffic throughout the metro area. Due to everyone trying to communicate with their cell phones, the networks shut down. Texting was the only way to communicate. I was tasked with picking up my fourth grade son and fifth grade niece from school and my neighbor's fourth grade twin daughters. Meanwhile, my neighbor was trying to pick up my ninth grade son, her ninth grade son, and her sixth grade son from multiple schools. I arrived at the elementary school to find out that all of the fourth graders had been released to walk to friends' houses, and the high school had stopped letting students go (although my ninth grader had gotten out and walked three miles to a friend's house).

That was about the time that I received a text from Kelly Garner. Kelly had reached out to me to see what he could do to help. I lead the Department of Public Services for our community, and our community has a tremendous volunteer network. Kelly Garner is one of those that will stop to help anyone. I told Kelly that right now he should go home and let our city workers clear the streets, because by this time the city roads were completely shut down due to the ice and snow, as well as the abandoned vehicles. Kelly unfortunately didn't listen to me. As you read Kelly's story in this book, I encourage you to count how many heroes have a part in the lives of their neighbors. It starts with Kelly's two boys starting the search of a lifetime. There are many opportunities in our lives to follow the example of Jesus Christ. Jesus says, "and the second is like it. You shall love your neighbor as yourself." Matthew 22:39. Kelly's story is a telling example of people loving their neighbor as themselves.

—Brian C. Davis, Director of Public Service.

* * *

The ice storm had hit with a vengeance and fury seldom experienced anywhere, much less here in the deep South. One inch of snow is a reason to close schools and businesses, but this was several inches of ice hitting suddenly and paralyzing the central part of Alabama, especially metropolitan Birmingham, trapping many people at work, in their cars on the side of the road, or taking refuge in stores and churches along the way. I had talked with my buddy Kelly Garner by e-mail and knew that he was heading out that morning for outpatient surgery just a few miles from his house. I hoped he had either made it back home before the ice hit or wound up staying at the hospital.

Fast forward to the next morning. Unable to navigate the forty-five-mile commute to work because of the ice, I was taking advantage of "sleeping in." I flipped on the news as I was lounging in bed and was vaguely hearing the story of a "good Samaritan" who had been helping stranded motorists—helping them push their cars over the mountain, buying cat litter to provide more tire traction on the ice, passing out snacks and water to those stranded—and then he had disappeared. In my half-awake state I remember thinking, "That sounds like something Kelly would be out doing." And then in one of those classic movie double-take moments, I sat bolt upright in bed and grabbed the remote to back up the story because it had just penetrated my mind that that was exactly who they had said was missing—Kelly Garner!

With that confirmation, I contacted my daughter so she would start praying and notify her group of praying friends; I notified my group of friends to do the same, and as the state leader of the diabetes educators, I notified the few of them whose contact information I had at home. A lot of prayers were going up for Kelly. The temperature had dropped to a low of nine degrees during the night—little chance of a person surviving out in that. A few hours later the news came that Kelly had been found alive at the bottom of a forty-foot ravine with head trauma and severe back injuries. It did not sound good. But prayers continued by many, many people.

This book is not only about Kelly's ordeal that night and his remarkable survival, but the amazing recovery and his miraculous journey to healing and thriving—a story you won't soon forget.

> —Sarah Joy Maxwell, BSN, RN, diabetes educator
> for a suburban hospital in central Alabama.

* * *

My sister Donna shared this about that night and what they experienced as I was nowhere to be found.

Tuesday January 28, 2014 is a day I have a hard time forgetting. About 10 pm, I was at home getting my clothes ready for work the next day when I received a phone call from my sister-in- law, Melissa, telling me that my brother Kelly was missing. I initially thought that she was joking with me. After a minute or two, I was convinced that this was no joke. All of a sudden I went into panic mode. I had this overwhelming sense of fear. All I could think was how I was going to get to Birmingham to look for him, someone has to look for him! He can't be out in 8 degree weather, it's just too dangerous. I couldn't help but think the worst. The weather was horrible with roads closed and there was no way to get to Birmingham this night. I called my sister Charlotte who lives in Birmingham and told her all the information I had from Melissa. She got the word out to the news stations and Facebook begging for help finding Kelly. Then I called my mother and other siblings. I think we were all in a state of shock, like how can this be happening? Feeling helpless I had my husband and stepson to lean on as we waited for any kind of good news we were hoping to hear. I kept up with Facebook, just hoping to read something that would give us an idea where he might be. We kept vigil all night into the morning hours waiting on any news. Finally about 8:30 the next morning, Melissa called and said that he had been found and he was alive! That was the best news that I had ever heard. My mom and siblings received this phone call and we all rejoiced at the news. I honesty fell to my knees in relief and gratitude thanking Jesus for this miracle of letting my brother be alive. I had no clue what his condition was. It was only that he was alive. Waiting on the roads to clear to where they were passable was the next hardest thing. All I could think of was getting to Birmingham and seeing him and touching him for myself. That was the moment that I actually felt like I could breathe a sigh of relief. He was in no means okay, but alive to tell about this horrible ordeal. I am just so thankful to God that he spared my brother's life that night.

* * *

My twin sister Shelly, from Maryville, TN added....

The ice storm of January 28. 2014, I received a phone call from my sister saying our brother was missing. "Missing?" I asked. "How can he be

45

missing?" I cried and prayed all night that he would be found alive & safe. I felt so helpless. I wanted to go help look for him but I was in another state battling the same ice storm. My twin brother was missing in the freezing, icy weather. The good Lord kept Kelly safe that night, there were so many praying for him. God wasn't finished with Kelly yet and He had a reason for keeping him alive.

Kelly had a long road to recovery and he never gave up. He pushed himself and worked hard with so much determination and drive to get better. Kelly is definitely a fighter!

I praise God every day that Kelly survived that awful night of January night, the night that changed our lives....and many, many others.

The Refiner's Fire

UAB/Spain Rehabilitation Hospital would now be my home for the next twenty-three days. UAB is the only level 1 trauma hospital in the state of Alabama and happens to be the largest employer in the state as well. It is a teaching hospital attached to the university campus on the south side of Birmingham. I was listed in critical condition in Neuro ICU where I stayed for ten days. I had shattered vertebrae and a nearly severed spinal cord. To complicate matters, I had also developed a brain bleed that had to subside before any surgery could take place to repair my back. (Not to mention I had also broken a scapula, big toe, and seven ribs that required a chest tube to help drain the excess fluid.) My injuries caused a massive hearing loss in one ear.

My surgeon explained that I had completely obliterated the vertebrae. In fact, he described it to me much like a pot roast dinner (warning: just skip the rest of this paragraph if you're squeamish!). He had to slice my muscles open to expose the vertebrae and be able to get to the broken pieces—which explains why my back had felt like Saran Wrap. There was a constant tugging and pulling going on. It was my muscles trying to find their right spot and settle in. I am in a constant struggle to this day to help the back muscles become stronger and able to take the wear and tear our everyday lives put our backs through. As gross as the procedure sounds, it worked.

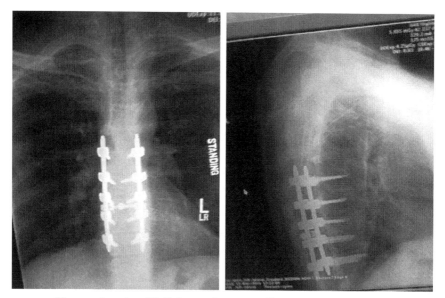

X-rays showing Kelly's newly surgically repaired vertebrae
with titanium rods and screws holding them in place

Escaping this near-permanent paralysis was listed as a "miracle" by my surgeon, Dr. William Neway. "God must have been looking over him," he said to my family.

Besides my persistent backache, which will never go away, the blow to my head caused traumatic brain injury or TBI. The pain caused me to want to be in a dark room with very low noise for hours and persisted for several more weeks. I couldn't see or talk with people for long. It was too painful to tolerate. I came out of the hospital with great respect for those who have backaches or have experienced a TBI. Therapists explained that though I have no scars to show or any outside bleeding of any kind, internally my brain had been tossed around like a bowl of Jell-O, which caused significant injury. Their explanation in lay terms helped me understand and accept my diagnosis.

The head injuries I sustained contributed to my loss of hearing in one ear and then in the other. Hearing aids are a must now.

They had me juiced up on some good stuff. My family said I was talking out of my head with funny anecdotes and things that were irritating me, but because of my condition I could not resolve them on my own. I understand Darius Rucker would have been proud of me. I had heard his song "Wagon Wheel" on the radio so much I had it stuck in my head, and several times they said that I would ask anyone who happened to be in the room to please remove that "wagon wheel" that was on my face. It set off a laughing storm for my caretakers.

I once told one of my nurses that I loved her father. Perplexed, she asked, "Who is my father?"

"Why," I said, "your father is George W. Bush, of course." Oh, the pleasures of modern medicine.

Because of the pain medication, I was not very aware of much of anything. I was in the hospital more than four days before I realized that I had broken my back and that I was in the NICU. It was not until the day after I came out of surgery that I understood what had been done to fix me. In fact, after leaving the hospital and rehab, I had a ton of appointments with doctors I had never met.

When meeting my back surgeon, Dr. Neway, and his team soon at my discharge, he walked into my exam room to take a look at my progress. I had to have a little fun with him and raised my shirt to expose my back and asked if seeing my back with the scars would remind him who I was. After all, he and his team were responsible for the beautiful work of art on my back that included a ten-inch scar. I said, "It's not fair that I did not have the chance to meet you prior to surgery. I want to see exactly what you used to piece me back together!" He then showed me samples of the two titanium rods and screws. I never knew surgeons had so much in common with carpenters! Though I was much improved, I was still no bionic man … yet. Nevertheless, I was healed enough to head home.

Kelly with Eiryn Mortellaro, RN, BSN, clinical care
coordinator and surgeon Dr. William Neway

This message came from my sister Donna as I was agitated and wanting to
leave the hospital: "Update on Kelly Garner ... he wants his shoes, socks,
pants, top and ball cap because he says that I'm 'busting' him outta here
today!! Bless him!!"

New Beginnings

My rehabilitation time was about ready to start. I first had to move to a step-down unit and prove that I could take a few steps. In other words, they began teaching me how to walk again. I almost laughed at the thought until I was asked to put my feet on the ground. Now, with my feet hitting the floor I saw the problem and laughed no more. Instead, I was now vomiting all over myself because of the excruciating pain shooting up my legs and down the lower half of my body. I now have a new deeper appreciation for the role our backs play in our everyday movement. It reminds me a lot of James Weldon Johnson's children's learning song we were taught growing up, "Dem Dry Bones": "The neck bone is connected to the head bone ... the toe bone is connected to the foot bone." I had no idea what kind of chaos happens when the bones aren't connected the right way!

On the bright side, some special visitors paid me a visit to encourage me. One of them was Bobby Humphrey, record-setting University of Alabama running back who went on to a four-year NFL career with the Denver Broncos before retiring in 1992. He came by with an invitation from his friend and ours, city employee Brian Davis. Brian was my friend who had gotten the ball rolling in my search from the city's end, and he too is a University of Alabama alum and a walk-on to the football program. Along with the visit came an autographed football from 'Bama head coach Nick Saban, 1992 National Championship–winning quarterback Jay Barker, Bobby, and a 2014 blue-chip defensive back signee to The Capstone, Bobby's son, Marlon. A lot of football talk took place in my room—a welcome diversion from the circumstances for me and everyone else in the room. I will cherish their gift like it was a million dollars.

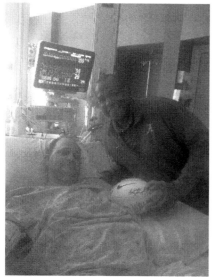 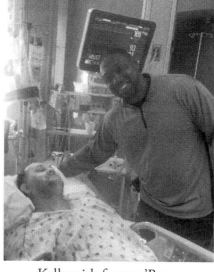

Kelly with former UA football
player Bobby Humphrey

Kelly with former 'Bama
star Antonio Langham

Another University of Alabama guest came by happenstance. My niece Katherine was at a local bar and grill enjoying the atmosphere and good times with her husband, Jim, when the local TV news break came on the bar's TV with an update and picture of me. Katherine overheard former 'Bama defensive back Antonio Langham say, "I want to shake the hand of my hero, Kelly Garner." She stepped into the conversation to tell him that she could make that happen because "He so happens to be my uncle." They exchanged phone numbers and met up the next morning at UAB Hospital where he too was a big hit. Antonio played with Jay Barker on the 1992 National Championship team that beat the University of Miami handily, and he also played pro ball with several NFL teams, including the Cleveland Browns, leaving the sport in 2000. Langham held a Tide team record of nineteen interceptions.

This was great medicine not only for me but also for all those who had a chance to get a picture made or just to meet with these fine individuals who gave of their time to share with others. Their visits created an enormous distraction for family, my visiting friends, and me. There were a lot of unknowns and a lot of standing and sitting around hoping for something to occupy time. Having them come by made time pass a bit faster.

The next process I went through in rehabilitation meant turning to the pros in physical therapy, occupational therapy, speech therapy, and neuropsychological evaluations. I was determined to heal. I would spend five grueling hours a day, for the next eight consecutive days, speeding up my walking and balance skills.

People from this city and state, and even many patients from around the country and overseas, have experienced the wonderful medical facilities we offer in Birmingham. Some have yet to understand how blessed we are with what we have here. With this care, I have been fortunate beyond reason. One of my stops I made was to the UAB Spain Rehabilitation Center. They have more than fifty years of experience. They have forty-nine beds that feature advanced, individualized care for people of all ages recovering from a broad variety of health problems. Dr. Robert Brunner and his staff of nurses, nurse practitioners, and therapists saw to my every need while at Spain. Their interdisciplinary treatment approach to patient care provides numerous health care workers from all areas of UAB. The physical therapy team encouraged me (insisted I needed) to get out of my bed and start conditioning myself. And I did.

Kelly with Dr. Robert Brunner, trauma doctor,
at a discharge news conference

I even set what to many around me looked like an unattainable goal: running a marathon! Trying to be reasonable, I decided to start first with a half-marathon and work my way up—once my rehabilitation got me to that point. It all began when I was watching the 2014 Mercedes marathon live on TV, with WBRC Fox6 Sports Reporter Sheldon Haygood describing the runners on the course while trailing in a Hummer. I sat in my bed on that Sunday morning and cried while watching, saying, "I will pull myself up out of this hospital bed, put these feet on the ground, and start this rehabilitation and run in the 2015 Mercedes Marathon." It wasn't until my therapy at Lakeshore Rehab later that I would truly begin to train toward that goal.

> *He heals the brokenhearted and binds up their wounds.*
> (Psalm 147:3)

While at Spain Rehab, I needed to walk the hospital hallways, learn to walk up and down steps and stairways, balance on one foot, get myself dressed, put on and lace up shoes, and even learn to go to the bathroom. I worked on some shoulder therapy to get my range of motion back once again. I was put through cognitive thinking skills that involved testing some basic everyday living skills like counting money, repeating the alphabet, and drawing pictures from memory, just for starters.

My mother, Millie, had put many individuals through these same exercises, as she worked for nearly forty years as a physical therapist assistant for Eliza Coffee Memorial Hospital in Florence. When she visited, she personally saw me work out and got to evaluate my own physical therapists, Candie Lambert and Alisa Korn, to see how they were conducting their business.

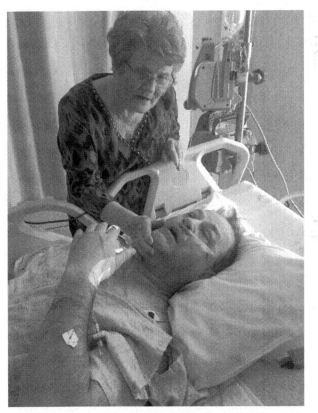

Kelly's mother, Millie, giving that loving motherly love touch

These women put me to the test! They worked tirelessly and diligently to get me through the process. I fought tooth and nail to push through to make this part of my hospital stay worth it and show that I was up and ready to get back to the real world. To better manage my own ordeal, I found comfort and satisfaction in encouraging other patients undergoing similar struggles. I think it added to the positive environment the therapists had already created. But at any rate, it helped me push on and progress faster than they had predicted, and I was moved ahead in the process of being discharged. With all the hard work, I was way ahead of schedule.

Now it was time for me to move on to my outpatient rehabilitation time at HealthSouth Lakeshore Rehabilitation Hospital, another example of a top-notch, devoted medical care facility offered here in the Magic City. HealthSouth's therapists conducted first-class business, as in the other facilities I got acquainted with. They directed all my extended physical therapy time.

For those who saw what I had to go through to learn to walk again, this is a testament to the professional abilities of the phenomenal staff at Lakeshore Rehab. All my therapists encouraged me not only to do my best but to dream big. So I decided to focus energy on my dreams of running a marathon. Though it may have sounded impossible at the time, running was the one sport that I felt I could still accomplish despite my diabetes. Plus, if I let anyone down, it would only be me, since it isn't a team sport.

As I was writing of *The Night That Changed Our Lives,* I had actually begun training for my first half marathon. My running coach, Danny Harelson, RRCA and AFAA Certified, gave me a quote from Teddy Roosevelt that reads: "Believe you can and you're halfway there." His advice resonated with a conviction I already had and may have been the reason I worked so hard to heal.

Eventually, my dream became reality 364 days from my release from the hospital. And to top off the miracle, the course took us just a few short city blocks away from UAB Hospital. There were members of my surgical team who were inspired enough that they, too, wanted to run with me. Some said, "If Kelly can do it, we should be there with him as well."

Kelly at Mercedes Marathon
February 2015
Photo by Jeri Fiinchum

Kelly at finish line

Kelly with surgeon William Neway after both
completed Mercedes Half-Marathon.
Photo by Jeri Fiinchum

Team 413–Gracerunner Ministries is the world's largest ministry for endurance athletes. Their primary mission is to share Christ with "whosoever" along their journey. The team is composed of anyone who wants to proudly display one of their running shirts that proclaims just "ONE MORE BREATH, ONE MORE STEP, ONE MORE MILE and FINISH LINE." This statement says it all for me—embodies everything I felt during my rehabilitating and training runs. The team utilizes the Scripture of Philippians 4:13—"I can do all things through Christ who strengthens me." I am honored to have worn this running shirt while running in numerous races.

Lakeshore Foundation was my final stop on the road to rehabilitation. Lakeshore Foundation is a nonprofit organization that serves people with physical disabilities throughout Alabama, across the country, and around the world. Since 1984, Lakeshore Foundation has helped advance and promote the impact of positive, long-term physical and emotional effects of physical fitness on people with disabilities. From infants to seniors, from injured soldiers to elite athletes, every participant is free to discover his or her own potential. Their mission is to "enable people with physical disabilities and chronic health conditions to lead healthy, active, and independent lifestyles through physical activity, sport, recreation, advocacy, policy, and research."

It has been an awesome sight to see our military men and women who have been injured participate in the Lima Foxtrot program. It is terrible that they are experiencing some anguishing trauma of their own while serving this country. These are the most severe cases one can imagine: brain injuries, internal trauma, amputations, and more. Some have the benefit of staying on campus at one of the cottages built specifically for disabled veterans. This is a well-deserved benefit that Lakeshore has been able to provide the veterans and their families.

It is humbling not only to see our veterans here but just to realize how fortunate I am when I see residents of metro Birmingham, just like myself, going through their own workouts to improve their everyday lives. Many have brought a smile to my face, and I give them a smile in return, hoping it will encourage them to carry on with the fight. They have been an inspiration to me. These individuals are from all walks of life, with all kinds of physical disabilities. Just to see them scratch together an ounce of courage is enough.

Lakeshore Foundation is also a US Olympic and Paralympic training site, preparing our nation's elite athletes to compete on the world stage.

My workouts were nothing compared to those of some I got to watch going through their exercises. I was able to use the weights to gain some good arm strength and build my core to a level where I would be able to run some good mileage. Lakeshore has an awesome therapy pool that is Olympic size. I was able to utilize the indoor track that serves a multipurpose role. Not only is it a walking track, but basketball courts there serve as home court to the Paralympic games.

When I wasn't formally training at the rehab center, I was still working hard at home to regain some normalcy. It took many weeks and months to be able to do some of the tiniest everyday things. I woke up during the night hours when I was used to having the nursing staff assist me. With my broken ribs not yet healed, I could not cough, sneeze, or laugh, much less go to the bathroom. I was not able to roll over in bed onto one side for months. The pain of just getting myself out of bed was immense.

Another condition I had developed from my temporal bone fracture but hadn't considered much until now was called BPPV (Benign Paroxysmal Positional Vertigo). As I have found, vertigo is not an easy thing to overcome. I have almost fallen to the ground after lying down or sitting down and then standing up.

A nagging pain I have had below the sternum area has lasted for months and was caused from the spine pressing up against the rib cage. The fall and the subsequent vertebrae fractures struck so severely that the injury caused a chronic bruise in my chest.

I still walk gingerly, afraid of stumbling and falling. With almost every step I take now, I recall how difficult it was to learn to walk again. I hope I never take this ability for granted and never have to experience that loss again.

My back pain will never go away—it will never be the same as it was prior to the accident. No one can tell me with a certainty what I should feel like or whether my back will return to something like a normal state. Only the grace of God strengthening me in my workouts and working through my therapists can help.

Ali Sanders, a personal trainer I have had the privilege to work out with, specializes in proactive rehabilitation for the back and for those like me who have experienced a setback. The proactive training is designed for those individuals who have a history of back issues. Ali has worked with me on using good posture in everything I do, something everyone should endeavor to do. She has been a godsend, a true blessing. She has taught me how to take better care of my body, while getting me back in condition. At the same time, she has instilled in me that this body of mine is God's temple. We are to take really good care of ourselves. We are on loan. She is a mother of three wonderful, very polite children: Rhett, Bella, and Carter. They are lots of fun to be around, definitely full of energy. I am proud to call her and her kids my friends.

Kelly with personal trainer Ali Sanders July 2014

Just like everything else in life, we succeed best when we work together. I'm grateful for the team of family, friends, and trained professionals who have come together to help me heal and prepare for the work of ministry I believe God has called me to do.

Pure Gold

What have I learned from all this? Bottom line, I know that God uses hard times to refine us. The fire takes out of our souls what doesn't need to be there, so that what remains shines brighter and purer as a reflection of God's glory. Though I wish the refining process wasn't so difficult, at the same time I am thankful for it because it has made me who I am today. I am grateful to still be here to share my story and, I hope, encourage other people as they walk through their trials too.

Many have asked if I had an angel or near-death experience while in the ravine. My answer is always a simple "No." I did have angels speak with me as plain as one would carry on a conversation, though. It happened when my father passed away of congestive heart failure more than thirty-five years ago. My source of comfort came through what I came to know as the power of prayer. While at my pastor's home, my sister Shelly and I were lying in our beds ready to go to sleep. I began a prayer, and as I dropped off to sleep, angels came over me to prep me for the bad news that my pastor's family was about to relay to us. The angels were comforting me and letting me know that they had taken my father to heaven to be with Jesus. They let me know that he was in a much better place and he was a "whole" man again.

Kelly with his father, Frank, 1979

But that was not the experience in the ravine. As strange as it may sound, as far as I know, it was peaceful, quiet, and still—but there was no "meet Jesus" moment or any discussions held with angels on that cold, dark January 2014 night. I like to think that angels did take care of me and helped me keep warm in the frigid weather—wrapping themselves around me, providing me with the security and comfort that I needed. Whatever the case, I've learned that, whether I am lying in a bed awaiting bad news or in a ravine awaiting help, God's grace has always been sufficient to carry me through.

That fateful night, I became known as "that missing Vestavia man" or the "good Samaritan." I even heard "snow angel." The one word that embarrasses me more than any other is "hero." I heard this repeatedly from my bedside and was so medicated that I could not express how upset I was at hearing this word used to describe what I and hundreds all over the city had done to help their neighbors and total strangers. I was upset because the men and women in law enforcement, fire and rescue, US military, and first responders all put their lives on the line every single day for all of us without hesitation. These are the true heroes. My diabetic issues caused me some problems on that particular night and brought undue attention to myself. Tears streamed down my face as I listened from my hospital bed, amazed at the love of God's people and the way He could use an ordinary person like me—weaknesses and all— to make a difference in this world.

Later, I heard people talking about the sacrifice I made serving others and how it made them reflect on the greatest sacrifice ever made to save others: Jesus Christ on the cross. I guess that when Jesus told His followers to "Take up your cross and follow Me," He was inviting each one of us to lay down our lives for others, just as He did for us. When we obey that call, others see Jesus in us. What a privilege! Not only that, but in the end, God has provided for my family and me tenfold. When all the dust cleared, the events had more clarity and meaning. I do believe that God had a purpose for me, though it took several months after being discharged from the. hospital for me to have that faith. I was told many, many times that God must have saved me for a reason—God provided the miracles that I was given because He definitely has more plans for me. Many said, "You need to write a book" or "We will be seeing you on a TV movie one day." One even predicted that I would be up and running a marathon one day.

> *And God raised us up with Christ and seated us with him in the heavenly realms in Christ Jesus, in order that in the coming ages he might show the incomparable riches of his grace, expressed in his kindness to us in Christ Jesus. For it is by grace you have been saved, through faith—and this not from yourselves, it is the gift of God—not by works, so that no one can boast. For we are God's workmanship, created in Christ Jesus to do good works, which God prepared in advance for us to do. (Ephesians 2:6–**10**)*

"When fear knocks on your door, send faith to answer." —Jesse Joseph

I do believe that God has saved me to share with others the hope they, too, can find in Him. The devil throws all of us in pits of different kinds. For me, it was a literal pit (in addition to a financial one). For others, it may be depression, or marriage failures, rebellious kids, lost loved ones, or a million other trials. But God is powerful enough to raise us up and put our feet on solid ground. In fact, a relationship with Him is the solid ground we all desperately need. What I did to help others that night was merely an extension of the love and care God has shown me. He inspires me to help others because that's who He is: the One who saves and rescues all of us. Though my ordeal has been long and hard, I have been blessed with an opportunity to share who Jesus is and the good He has in store for those who trust Him.

Kelly's photo hanging in Spain Rehabilitation Hospital's Wall of Courage

Kelly giving presentation as surprise guest speaker at UAB Trauma Symposium

Mike Shofner, neighbor and rescuer, when asked if he knew how I got to the bottom of the ravine, said, "I'd be surprised if he could tell you. Especially after being out there all night. I haven't figured out how he stayed alive." Shofner went on to say, "There is a story ahead of him somewhere." They were definitely surprised that I was not frozen to death. He was correct when he felt that there is more of a story to follow my near-death episode.

I believe that faith is not knowing what the future holds, but knowing God, who holds our future. It is a relationship that never ends. Our time on earth is a gift from God. When people ask me, "Why would God do something like this to a guy like you?" I always answer that we are not asking the right question. Instead, we should trust Him in the situation and ask what He wants us to learn about who He is and what He'd like for us to do in the situation. Great peace comes when we realize we are not in control of our timeline. God is in control and operates on His time. The problem is that none of us like to wait on God's timing.

I recently read a book given to me by a friend of my sister Charlotte. Her friend's pastor wrote it. He tells about his venture into the ministry and how slow out of the gates it was for him and his family. They had sacrificed a lot to move to Atlanta and start a church. But not just any church. His desire was to be a megachurch pastor. The slow start in the growth of his congregation was just the beginning. This pastor really wanted to preach in front of lots of people. After consulting and praying with his spiritual prayer partner, he found that his prayers were "Where is my megachurch, God?" His friend had to set the prayer moving in another direction, and that was to pray to God to bring him his megachurch when it was His time.

Writer Nishan Panwar tells us "God will always give us what is best for us at the right time. We just shouldn't give up on Him even when it seems we aren't getting what we so much love or want now." So, you see, I too had to learn how to pray to God and realize that we are on His time.

One day, while lying in my hospital bed, I had a visit from a national TV news magazine producer. He had caught word of my accident and wanted to gather the information of what had happened straight from my mouth. I joked that I was so heavily medicated that I might have shared lots of personal things that I should not have been sharing with a complete stranger. Months passed, and I had not heard from any of these individuals from New York. I had determined that it just wasn't as glamorous a story as they had hoped. Perhaps there was too much God involved in my story.

But my story is one between God and me and how He has used me and these miracles to share with others His love and blessings. While there might not have been any miraculous feats on my part to extract myself out of this ravine, He certainly has kept me here to share His undying love for all and the greatest gift of all-time to be spent in Heaven with Him.

Many, Many Thanks

There were times when I would walk into a room someplace and people would take a hard look at me, not knowing my name perhaps but recognizing my face as "that person" who had gone through a trying time during our snow and ice storm. Eventually I would start to hear "You're that guy." It was definitely a surreal time for me. I had so many people reminding me what a blessing I had been to them and that I had a lot to be thankful for and that God had plenty more for me to do. It still took me a while to come to grips with everything that had happened. More than a year later, I am finally getting close to wrapping my arms around it, putting the final pieces of the puzzle together after gathering all the information from friends and family.

Just to show how wonderful God is, even in time of peril, He brought me back together with my best friend after a misunderstanding that had lasted more than eight years. We had been friends since early high school days, and I had the honor to serve as best man in his wedding twenty-seven years ago. His lovely wife worked not too far away from UAB Hospital when my accident took place. Though my friend was away on business during the ordeal, his wife immediately came to support my wife and the emotional trauma she was experiencing. Her act of love in simply being there and offering my wife encouragement and a shoulder to cry on mended the brokenness between our families and united us again as the close friends we are now.

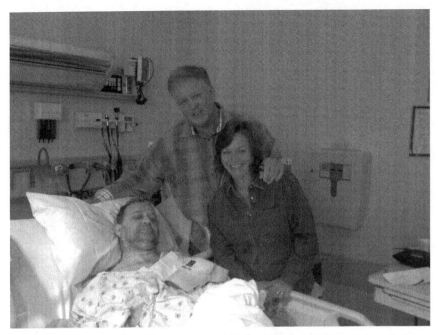

My friends, Roger and Robin Rich visiting

This is just one of many countless stories of God's loving mercy showing off in good fashion.

My trauma team had encouraged me to read how my life touched many, yet take it in only a little bit at a time. Facebook and Twitter were a part of helping save my life. When I say prayer warriors, this wasn't just in my neighborhood, church, city, or state. My name reached all around the world. I received get-well wishes from all fifty states and five different countries, including Valentine's cards from a group of school children in Spain. Kaire Netherland Morrissey's daughter, Henna Grace, one of those children, is in Sue Bosler's fourth-grade class. The school is DGF Elementary on the Naval Station in Rota, Spain. I received messages from individuals from all over the country who saw my story on their local TV news. All of this from perfect strangers. It is amazing to witness how God does answer the call to prayer.

Valentines Cards from Rota, Spain

We received a message from a lady who had not talked with her brother in quite a while over a fight they had. After what she saw my sisters and brother do for me at a time when I needed them the most, she realized how isolated she and her brother had become and was ashamed at how their relationship had languished. She then reached out to him with an olive branch, and they have remained in contact ever since. My calamity seems to have had positive effects on this family and similarly helped many others.

This is a message to my sister Charlotte from Todd Austin, January 30, 2014: "Char—it shows us that sometimes things are way out of our control and totally in God's. I have learned that in life, sometimes things make no sense but I am constantly shown the ability of God to provide when things seem 'out of sorts' to us. God took care of him in a mighty way. I am thrilled at the testimony that will come from it *when* he is well, not if. Keep us updated. Praying for him!"

This one from a Royal Ambassador (Baptist Boys program-ministry) Summer Camp Counselor friend of mine, Jonathan Askins: "Dude, I am so thankful you were found alive! What a great impact you've made on people! If I had a wife or child on that highway that you were on, I would have hoped someone like you would be there to help them if needed. Thanks for showing the Christ in you and help others … now take care of yourself and get better. I want to hear the whole story when you get better. Your Brother, Little Jon."

Jonathan continues with another note: "Kelly, the 'Brotherhood' of RA Counselors from 'the good ole days' will be lifting you in prayer this morning. Inside joke for Kelly … lots of Tuna Fish sandwiches on the way!! Stay strong!"

Another one sent by Jeanie Mimi Wallace says: "Thank you for the update on your brother who is a real hero. Although I have never met him, I am so inspired by his selfless act of compassion and I pray daily for his complete recovery. God bless and keep you and when he is well enough please let him know how many hundreds of thousands of lives he has touched by his heroism and please tell him that his story has inspired many more! All God's blessings on you during this difficult time."

And this missive comes from friend and former colleague Amy Rae Kennedy: "I wanted to share a personal story with you and your family. To say my relationship with God has been upside down the last few years is an understatement, to my embarrassment. Over the last week I have found myself hitting my knees and praying. Attended church yesterday for the first time in a few years. Getting back to where and who I want to be. I owe this to Kelly. He is a miracle who has brought people together who don't even know each other. My continued prayers for his healing and all of his family."

Some even mentioned that I have no idea how God used my accident to bring the entire Vestavia Hills community together as a whole. I do know now that I have a better appreciation for the city that I have called home for thirty years and for my wife, a lifelong resident. I was recognized by our local monthly paper, *Vestavia Voice*, as 2014 Community Member of the Year. Votes were taken through their website. Vestavia Hills is full of people making a difference in our community, and *Vestavia Voice* wanted to give the many citizens nominated for this award the recognition they deserve. Many wonderful individuals were up for this award, and I was proud to have been nominated and placed in the same category as these neighbors of mine.

Kelly with sponsors of HR338 Phillip Pettus and Jack Williams

Alabama Governor Robert Bentley poses for a photo with Kelly Garner at the state Capitol, Thursday, June 4, 2015, in Montgomery. Mr. Garner was presented an Alabama House Resolution for being a Good Samaritan who helped people in last year's ice storm in Birmingham. He was hospitalized for close to a month because he injured himself helping others that day. (Governor's Office, Jamie Martin)

Kelly and his family
Photo Credit Governor's Office, Jamie Martin

Kelly standing in State House Gallery

Representatives acknowledging myself in the gallery.

Photo Credit, Dionne Whetstone, Photographer,
Alabama House of Representatives.

Some things and some people come along in life that you just can't forget. That thing and that individual for me was the franchise owner of a local Philly Connection Sandwich shop. Sunel Merchant is a native of Bombay, India, who moved to the States in 1999 and went to work for a software company whose offices were located in one of the World Trade Towers in New York. He was on the forty-ninth floor when the planes hit and was able to make it down safely. A lot of bad memories are etched in his mind, but some of the good that emerged was what the first responders did for him and the many others who were rescued alive.

He recalls vividly the looks on faces of the firemen going up the stairwells to do their job. For some, it would be their last call to make. When he decided to leave New York after a merger and subsequent layoff, he packed his family up and moved to Alabama, where his cousin had resided for many years.

He found his home here when he found the warm Southern hospitality that his family received. That was when he opened up his franchise. He and his wife made a corporate decision to give back to first responders in his community on the day of remembrance of 9/11 by feeding those who do what they do as emergency personnel and who give of themselves daily, selflessly.

When the story of my accident reached the community head-on, he selected a day to benefit my "medical fund" and donate proceeds on this day's sales to this fund. This a good example of an incredible family who have embraced the American culture of giving and doing for others. Sunel is a dynamic speaker who has a fascinating story to tell. You, too, would be mesmerized at his presentation of his survival of the terrorists' attack in NYC.

The Merchants' daughter, Saloni, was an eighth grader at Auburn Junior High. She penned me a beautiful note. She shared my story with her classmates who also wrote notes of well wishes.

> Dear Mr. Garner, My name is Saloni Merchant. I am 13 years old. I found out what happened on that January night and

felt like everyone should know what you went through. So I went to my school and told my friends what had happened to you and the reaction was crazy. So crazy and touched with emotion many began to cry. I suggested that we should make a book of well wishes. I let everyone be creative and to write whatever you would tell him in person. May your life be better than it was. I hope you and your family are always together and have a good time together. All we wanted to do was to say thank you for your bravery.

She added some additional notes to go along with this opening message:

Everything in life is temporary so if things are going bad don't worry they can't last forever. The key to our success rests in people like you, who embody the spirit of greatness by saying, 'Yes I can, and so can you!' Thanks for your inspiring dedication and tremendous example to the world. Thank you for being so generous, thoughtful and so true. And thank you most of all for just being you.

How prophetic can a thirteen-year-old be? It was a beautifully written note from Saloni and her classmates she calls "The Crew."

This is a note that my twin sister Shelly had shared about a night she had with me. My family had "night duty" with me and swapped nights with one another. This was her night.

I'm really enjoying "night shift" in the Neuro ICU with Kelly Garner tonight. He just wants me sitting right by his bed so we can talk. He asked me what day it was. When I told him it was Tuesday, February 4, he quietly said … a week ago tonight. We both teared up just thinking about what he endured that night in that cold, dark 40' ravine. I reminded him that God was with him that night and He wasn't finished with him. Treasuring my time with this guy.
♥ ♥ ♥

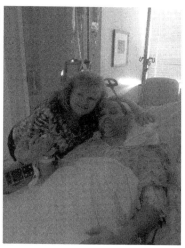

| Kelly & Shelly July 1989 | Shelly with Kelly @ UAB Hospital February 2014 |

This is a message in which my sister Charlotte gave thanks for the thoughts and prayers:

> Convinced that it was the grace of God that sent His protection & mercies & angels for my brother Kelly while he spent 14+ hours in the 8 degree cold, was severely injured, that he didn't aspirate on the blood he was throwing up, that he didn't go into a diabetic coma, that his spinal cord didn't snap in two when one of his thoracic vertebra completely obliterated leaving him paralyzed, and the hemorrhage in his brain has not killed him.
>
> He's not out of danger yet, so please continue to mention his name. He is having surgery [UPDATE: soon, yet-to-be-determined time today] on that vertebra at UAB in Birmingham. Will try to update when we can. Facebook has been a wonderful prayer chain, and I want to personally thank each & every one of you when I can. Love y'all!!—Feeling blessed.

And there were so many more touching words of encouragement:

> Continued prayers for you and your family ... I have
> received calls from all over Alabama ... from the Shoals,
> Birmingham, Huntsville, Mobile, Montgomery, and as far
> South as Pensacola! You are loved by soooooo many, and
> each one is praying for you ... and praising God! Two calls
> today, my friend and co-worker for many years ... and those
> calls continue on a daily basis! If I can be of assistance, in any
> way ... call or text! You have my number:>) LA.

> —Lee Ann Tyler, a friend and former colleague of mine

This one coming from Bill Averill; "Kelly, I know you are having a tough
time and hate the attention, but sometimes you just have to take it all in
and be glad because you have touched so many people. I hope I would
do the same as you but it is easy to just do nothing and pretend it is all
someone else's problem."

Kelley Griffith Shore shared:

> Sending out prayers and prayer requests tonight for Kelly
> Garner and his family. For those who are blessed to know
> Kelly, you know he's one of those special people in life whom
> everybody loves and adores!! He is a rare gem. I wish I was
> close by to give you a big bear hug Kel. You are a fighter
> my friend and your heroic story does not surprise me—
> always genuinely concerned and willing to help others. To
> Kelly's family—I worked with Kelly at ADC and he has
> touched so many of us and is loved by many!!! Thank you for
> sharing these updates. I'll be praying for you and your family
> tomorrow Kel!! BIG HUGS!!!!

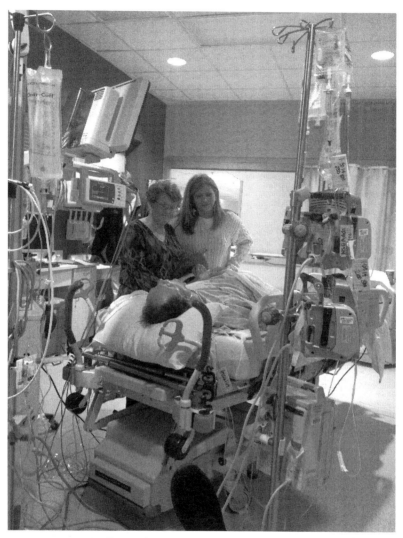

Kelly in the UAB NICU January 2014

Kelly in Neuro ICU—surgery on T6 busted vertebra has been RESCHEDULED for 10:15 am Friday. Please keep him in your prayers!! Thanks, friends!

"Hey Kel! Just checking in to say hi. Your story is still so surreal to me. ... literally like a scene out of a movie. Your strength is amazing and I'm so happy that you are here with us! Hang in there Kel and keep fighting the good fight! XO" added Kelley Griffith Shore, just a few days away from my discharge.

> Kelly Garner I have been a fan of yours ever since one of the first times that I ever met you in one of my pharmacies. As quick as we are all to say "it won't happen to me" to myself and also to everyone else, it can and it does. Unexpectedly how something can change the life of not just one person, but the life of the family as well as the life of friends. Kelly Garner your story has proven to be nothing short of a miracle in its own right. With everything that you personally are going through, I also want to give props to Melissa Garner and y'all's two boys for persevering through times like these. There will never be words to describe what y'all as an intermediate family have been through. Keeping up with your story through social media would not have been possible without thanks to Charlotte Garner Carter. It's been a Long and Winding Road, but with all the loneliness and crying, and without keeping you waiting too long, it led you back to your door. My gratitude for those who had a hand in locating you and for those that were responsible in caring for you. Hope your weekly activities become easier with every passing day. Don't hesitate to call if you ever need anything. Love you man!
>
> —Tim Peterson

"You are an inspiration to all of us. I'm so honored to be your friend. You're in my prayers. Be at peace knowing you are right where you are supposed to be! HUGS." (Stacey Sarros Hornyak)

"Thanks for the update. I'm still in awe of how our God is still in the miracle business today! I know He will use you in some incredible way with this for the work of His kingdom. Keep up the hard work to get stronger and better. You are an inspiration to so many!!" (Brenda Deen)

"Kelly I too have been in your position ... I could go on with all kinds of clichés and what not but the best thing I can say is walk by faith and not by sight. It's easier said than done especially when one is worried about the roof over their head and insurance etc. But, all that worry just makes your health worse and accomplishes nothing. If we are to believe there is no greater love than the man who would lay down his life for his friend I HAVE to believe something wonderful and good is there for a man so deserving." (Chris Wilkerson)

This is another message from Chris that I received after the Mercedes Half Marathon. She just about sums up how things occurred from her perspective.

> Rev. Chris' Sunday Sermon. The man who you are reading about should be dead. Scientifically and with all my experience he should absolutely without a doubt be in a wood box in the ground. A granite or marble marker inscribed here lies Kelly Garner. One fateful Tuesday night a year ago (Jan 2014) came a rare ice storm. Oh the weather people said it wouldn't be bad but then as is often the case everyone woke up and nothing happened. Everyone went to school and work as normal and then ... ... Then IT BEGAN TO SNOW AND SLEET. Seeing it was going to get bad quickly employers and schools let out. Problem was they all let out at the same time causing gridlock. And then over 50k motorists got stranded on Alabama roadways. Stranded just a short way from home. Kelly could have walked home ... He could have been warm and dry ... his wife would have been so thrilled. But instead being a diabetic he knew from fb posts that some of the stranded motorists were also sick folks and needed to be checked on. And so Kelly began walking from fb post need to fb post need. He helped many that night and then disappeared. A year ago he laid in subzero temperatures all night having fallen down a ravine in a diabetic coma. Breaking his back and a few ribs, having a stroke and can't remember what else ... But should have died. After lying

out there for 13–15 hours in a raging ice storm before his neighbors found him in under 2 hours and his face and name were circulating on the a.m. news. But sadly, he should have absolutely without a doubt been dead. This morning he ran half a marathon; let me say that again HE RAN A HALF MARATHON IN A RESPCTABLE TIME NO LESS. Now I'm not what you'd call a religious person. As a minister I'm definitely more of a spiritual person ... CALL IT A HIGHER POWER, KARMA BEING REPAID TO A KIND AND DECENT SOUL. CALL IT WHAT I DO. A MIRACLE. REALLY DOESNT MATTER BECAUSE IN SPITE OF OVERWHELMING ODDS ... A GUY WHO WE SHOULD BE VISITING IN A CEMETERY JUST RAN A HALF MARATHON. Proud of you Kelly.

Our neighbor, Sheila, reached out to those who wanted to provide meals for my family, both while I was hospitalized and when I returned home. She spearheaded this effort and stayed on top of it, making sure we had what we needed, and if we didn't, she saw to it that it happened. We had food brought to our home for about two months. It is these types of neighbors that we are blessed to have in Vestavia Hills. Through their efforts, we were able to find out what neighborly love truly is. I was able to meet and greet many of our neighbors on our sidewalks as I strolled through, hoping to get my strength back once again and working on my own personal rehabilitation. I met many people I had not met before. Some told stories of what they experienced during the storm, and others shared how they were out helping to search for me. There have been lots of hugs and well wishes, laughs shared, and some tears shed.

State law, because of the injuries I sustained, forbade me from driving for six months after my accident. When I did get my wheels back, I dished out some hugs of my own to employees at a few of our local businesses that I patronize. It started with one of my first visits to one of our local businesses that I visit regularly. After seeing me enter the store, one of the clerks recognized me. She came from behind the counter to give me a hug. I was so thankful and just wanted to reach out and hug many others, after she inspired me by giving me that first hug. She showed me what I meant to them and our community.

By being able to drive once again, I knew I had lots to get caught up on, and it helped relieve Melissa from chauffeuring me around from one doctor visit to another, and then on to the local Walgreens for medication pickup. Rehabilitation was one of those chores, too. Those trips were a part of our weekly schedule. It was one visit after another. This schedule became a routine for us.

During my rehabilitation, people from all walks of life encouraged me with their kind words:

"He's been a hard worker, and everyone's liked working with him, and … his help didn't really stop with what he was doing that night, "Brunner said. "He's helping all the other patients in the gym too, and motivating them and doing things like that. It's been a great experience for all of us."

Physical therapist Alicia Korn said that Garner was "amazing."

"From day one, he came in highly motivated, ready to work, never let pain or fatigue affect him," she said. "He just kept going and doing whatever we told him to do."

The whole staff saw me as a "hero," she said, "because he tried to help others the day of the storm and put them ahead of himself."

Candice Lambert, a physical therapy student, said it was a "great opportunity" to get to know and work with Garner. "He was just an awesome man," she said.

Kelly with members of his occupational therapy team Blake Jesse and Brittany Harris

Kelly and his physical therapy crew, Alisa Korn, PT, DPT, CSCS and Candice Lambert Uselton, PT, DPT

But I wasn't the only one to get attention. I was so proud of my boys and all our friends who helped me on that night and who were recognized at the Vestavia Hills City Council meeting in March 2014, for their bravery and stamina too. I have certainly been blessed with an awesome neighborhood and community. Thanks, Brian Davis, for this invite and for spotlighting those who sacrificed a lot to rescue me. Brian spotlighted Tyler and Mitchell for their take-charge attitude and for their desire to do what they had to do to locate where their dad might have been on that January night.

Now it is time to give out a few shameless plugs to some companies whose items were with me on my fateful night in the snow and ice. I was layered from head to toe with thermal underwear and top, another long sleeve undershirt, flannel shirt, boot socks, gloves, toboggan, and LL Bean boots. These boots almost outlasted me that night. I have had these Bean boots for more than thirty years.

I had on my favorite winter jacket that day. It was the best winter jacket I have ever owned and the warmest. Eddie Bauer has always been a wonderful retailer. I bought it in Kansas City, Missouri, while on business in 1995, during a freakish winter storm that was their first recorded snowfall before

Halloween. Of course I had to be there for their record-breaking weather moment. This jacket had to be cut off of me for the fire medics to get me all hooked up to IVs and a blood pressure monitor and check for injuries unseen by the eyes. It was cut up so much that it had to be totaled.

When word got to Eddie Bauer about what had happened to me and my jacket, they graciously replaced it with a couple of free jackets to say thanks for my loyalty and for the effort I gave to the community. They did mention that they believe the new, replaced jackets will serve me very well in my future adventures. Of course, this prompted those who know me well to roll their eyes and say that Kelly will not be having any more adventures like the one that got this jacket in deep trouble in the first place. I must say that this was a very nice way to keep me as a loyal customer. Thanks, Eddie Bauer!

I had on my only pair of jeans that night. They were Wrangler jeans, and they survived without a scratch or tear on them. What a rough and rugged pair to have handled all that I put them through on that night. I still wear them proudly today.

My Apple smartphone was with me, but without a protective case of any kind. I had been having very short-term battery life, and this was not a night when I needed this to happen. My kids had named my phone a dumb smartphone because of the battery problem I had been having. After I had been reported as missing and after my family had repeatedly phoned me to no avail, the police attempted to "ping" my phone—meaning to pick up my signal off of the nearest cell tower. This technique would make it possible for law enforcement to locate me. By the time all of this was becoming apparent, my phone had already expired. No battery, no signal, the phone was dead. It was found later the afternoon that I was pulled out of the ravine. It lasted in this Arctic winter weather longer than I did. It was still there in the woods and was in working condition once it was charged. I am still using this phone today.

My jacket might have been totaled and my back forever altered, but one good thing I did come out of the hospital with was a newfound kinship with Jesus Christ. I have more inner peace about things than I have ever felt before. The dislike, contempt, or disgust I might have had toward others has gone away. In more ways than one, it has not been easy getting back to the "real" world!

Counting—and Being—the Blessings

This just might sum it all up for many of us. Jesse Joseph writes: "You may not understand today or tomorrow, but eventually God will reveal why you went through everything you did." I am learning this almost daily. I have heard many stories from individuals who have shared with me how they have a newfound faith in what God has in store for all of us.

God gave us a heart to love with. God gave us the ability to create heaven on earth, not hell. I don't have time to worry about who doesn't like me … I'm too busy loving the people who love me for who and what I am. And for those who don't, I just pray that one day they will come to see God's love for them.

> *We live by faith, not by sight.* (2 Corinthians 5:7)

When I go on my many runs and walks, the route that I take puts me in the exact location of my collapse. I have found myself using this site as a prayer altar. It is a place to reflect on all that has happened during this time of my misstep, my recovery and rehabilitation time. Usually by the time I am done reminiscing, I am weeping and blubbering, thankful for God's grace and allowing me this time of healing that I have gone through.

When I was laid off from my job after thirteen years of service back in 2013, I would have never guessed that it was a blessing in disguise. Though I daily sought work and tried to reenter the work force, God kept shutting the door. Now I know that the peaceful feeling that I have had these past few years was allowed to grow because I was not in the rat race of a heavy workload and stressful week of work. Once the accident happened, I didn't have the stress of trying to get back to work. I knew that most, if not all, of my "extra" time needed to be spent rehabilitating. As for bills, my family and I simply trusted the Lord.

In God's providence, the company that laid me off kept me on the company-paid medical insurance. Without this benefit, available to me through the company plan, we would have been devastated into bankruptcy. Hospital bills totaled well over $130,000.

There have not been any harsh feelings about the massive, companywide layoff. I know that God does have a purpose for my life, and His will *will* be done. When the right opportunity comes knocking, I will be ready to take that call. One door has closed, and another will open sooner or later. My greatest work right now is prayer.

Our budget has become much tighter than it has ever been. We have been humbled but in the process blessed beyond measure. Once I read a bulletin board at the hospital where I was receiving treatment that said, *"Count your blessings instead of counting sheep."* It was exactly what we were learning to do.

Not having that monthly paycheck has definitely been a challenge, but we are not the only family facing this trial. Through this humbling process, I have learned to respect those who have been displaced and are now fighting, scraping together whatever they can to feed their families and house them. It makes me appreciate every little thing I have even more. Remember, what we do have is each other and the love we can pass along. When I start to consider each one, God's amazing grace seems even greater.

One of those amazing things happened when a "Kelly Garner Medical Fund" was established to help offset my hospital costs. The fund helped us pay the bills that were not covered under our insurance plan. Perfect strangers gave money to another stranger, anonymously. I was heartbroken not being able to thank these individuals personally. Instead, I relied on social media once again—this time to offer universal thanks to everyone who has cared for me and my family.

> *Therefore go and make disciples of all nations, baptizing them in the name of the Father and of the Son and of the Holy Spirit, and teaching them to obey everything I have commanded you. And surely I am with you always, to the very end of the age.* (Matthew 28:19–20)

God, too, has provided me not only the time to recover and heal my wounds, but also the time needed to get *The Night That Changed Our Lives* together, so I can share what a privilege it has been for me and my family to be used—and blessed—by God through these trials. This has been an incredible journey that I pray will bless all who read this book, my labor of love and appreciation, for all that God and His people have done in my life. With apparently nine lives and counting, I am more intent than ever to run the race God has set before me in a way that honors Him. He has been with me every step of the way through this journey. I am forever grateful that He has.

An awakening has taken place. What it has boiled down to is this: I shouldn't, nor will I, allow this opportunity to slip away. After spending time near death, for the second time—after all that I just went through and the miracles—I figured it was finally time for me to listen. I might very well have squandered the chance after my horrible bone-crushing accident ten years ago. Not this time: There is this thing called a new lease on life for a reason. I believe the events of Snowmageddon were God's wake-up call, and it was time for me to answer. I want to be the kind of disciple and leader who actually follows Him as He works out even pain and suffering for my good.

There is a short poem that I have had in my possession for years called *Today*, the author unknown. It has always touched my soul—and I hope it encourages you, too:

> There are two days in every week about which we should not worry, two days that should be kept free from fear and apprehension.
>
> One of these days is Yesterday with its mistakes and cares, its faults and blunders, its aches and pains. Yesterday has passed forever beyond our control.
>
> All the money in the world cannot bring back Yesterday. We cannot undo a single act we performed. We cannot erase a single word we said. Yesterday is also beyond immediate control.
>
> Tomorrow's sun will rise, either in splendor or behind a mask of clouds—but it will rise. Until it does, we have no stake in Tomorrow, for it is yet unborn.
>
> This leaves only one day—Today. Any man can fight the battles of just one day; It is only when you and I add the burdens of those two awful eternities—Yesterday and Tomorrow—that we break down.
>
> It is not the experience of Today that drives men mad; it is remorse or bitterness for something that happened Yesterday and the dread of what Tomorrow may bring.

This has always stuck with me when trying to think about those dreadful bygone days or the upcoming events on our calendars. It is hard to overcome fear, but we must not let these stressors infect our attitudes, robbing us of the joy Jesus wants us to experience by trusting Him. Put the past behind you, and allow God to strengthen you for what happens today.

> *Be still before the LORD and wait patiently for him; do not fret when men succeed in their ways, when they carry out their wicked schemes .... But the Lord laughs at the wicked, for he knows their day is coming.* (Psalm 37:7, 13)

I encourage you when waking up in the mornings, brush aside any grumpiness and smile as you sip that first cup of coffee and thank the Lord for giving you one more day to enjoy Him on this earth. Rain or shine, let His love shine into your soul and out through a smile on your face.

Poster that hung in all of my rooms, given to me by Mary Kathryn, daughter of friends Kelly & Joey Bolton.

Think about what the Lord can bring you today in the form of a miracle, a blessing to share with others, or how you can give back to Him. Give each family member one big hug with a smile on your face as you each go in different directions. Leave them with good thoughts and that smile on your face. You never know when it is your time, and I now always want that hug and smile to be a lasting memory. Bessie Anderson Stanley reminds us to "live well, laugh often, and love much."

God bless each of you in your pursuit of happiness, and may God be in the forefront of whatever it is you are doing.

Works Cited

"Believe You Can, You Are Halfway There – Theodore Roosevelt Life Inspirational Quotes Poster." *We Heart It.* Teddy Roosevelt, n.d. Web. 20 Feb. 2015.

Brown, Leon. "God Gave You a Heart to Love With, Not to Hate with." N.p., n.d. Web.

Chambers, Jesse. "AL.com." *AL.com.* N.p., 21 Feb. 2014. Web. 21 Feb. 2014. <http://www.al.com/>.

Doss, Suthandra. N.p., n.d. Web. 07 May 2015.

Helms, Russell. "60 Hikes within 60 Miles, 2nd Edition." N.p., n.d. Web.

James Weldon Johnson. *Dem Dry Bones.* N.d. Vinyl recording.

Joseph, Jesse. N.p., n.d. Web.

Myers, Kevin, and John C. Maxwell. *Homerun: Learn God's Game Plan For Life And Leadership.* New York City: FaithWords, 2014. Print.

"A Note From:." *Welcome to TEAM 413!* N.p., n.d. Web. 3 Mar. 2015. <http://www.team413.org/>.

N.p., n.d. Web. 3 Mar. 2015. <www.lakeshore.org>.

Panwar, Nishan. "God Will Always Give Us What Is Best for Us at the Right Time. We Just Shouldn't Give up on Him Even When It Seems We Aren't Getting What We so Much Love or Want Now." *Search Quotes*. N.p., n.d. Web. 07 May 2015.

Reagan, Ronald. N.p., 4 Dec. 2014. Web.

Robinson, Carol. "AL.com." *AL.com*. N.p., 29 Jan. 2014. Web. 29 Jan. 2014. <http://www.al.com/>.

Stanley, Bessie A. "Live Well, Laugh Often, Love Much." *Quotes and Sayings*. N.p., n.d. Web. 05 Feb. 2015. <http://www.searchquotes.com/>.

Stanley, Charles. "In Touch – May 7, 2015." *Crosswalk.com*. N.p., n.d. Web. 07 May 2015.

"UAB – The University of Alabama at Birmingham – Home." *UAB – The University of Alabama at Birmingham – Home*. N.p., n.d. Web. 03 Mar. 2015. <http://www.uab.edu/>.

Wooden, John. "Famous Quotes." *BrainyQuote*. Xplore, n.d. Web. 20 Mar. 2015. <http://www.brainyquote.com/>.

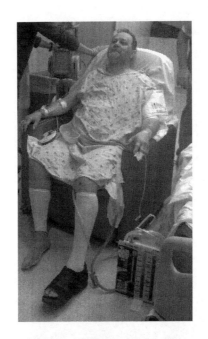

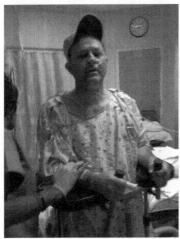

43881756R00073

Made in the USA
Lexington, KY
15 August 2015